Landscape Architecture **01**

the world of environmental design

Landscape Architecture 01

atrium
international

AUTHOR	Francisco Asensio Cerver
PUBLISHING DIRECTOR	Paco Asensio
PROJECT COORDINATOR	Carolina Gallego
PROOFEADING	Amber Ockrassa
GRAPHIC DESIGN	Mireia Casanovas Soley

PHOTOGRAPHERS

Maxwell Anderson (*Neve Zedek Plaza*); Dixi Carrillo, Hargreaves Associates, Jim Heidrich, David Walker (*IBM Solana*); F. Bertin, Atelier Cube (*La Garance*); Mick Hales (*Disney's Dixie Landings Resort*); Nahoiro Ito and the Pension Walfare Service Corporation (*GreenPia Tsunan*); Archeon, C. Beunder (*Archeon*); Efteling (*Efteling*); Taizo Furukawa, Hirotsugu Takahashi, Masafumi Koda (*Parque España*); Sue Bennett (*General Hitchcock Highway*); Tatsuo Hayashi (*Shirotori Garden*); Joan Mundó (*Clàstics*); Andy Goldsworthy (*The Wall, Oak Tree, Elm Leaves, Red Pool, Balanced Rocks*), Ingrid Voth-Amslinger (*Himmelstreppe, Wachstumsspirale*); Jacques Simon (*Leonardo da Vinci, Marianne, Le Drapeau de l'Europe, Messages...*); David Nasch (*Wooden Boulder, Black Dome, Divided Oaks*), Alessandro Gui, Alexandra Boulat (*Restructuration de l'Avenue des Champs-Élysées*); Seiichi Motoki, Shinkenchik-sha (*Police Box*), Wilfried Dechau (*Schiedgraben und Hirschgraben in Schwäbisch Hall*); Georges Descombes, Françoise Goria, Hervé Laurent (*Voie Suisse. L'itineraire genevois*)

© FRANCISCO ASENSIO CERVER, 1996

REGISTERED OFFICE

Ganduxer 115, 08022 Barcelona. Spain
Tel. (93) 418 49 10
Fax. (93) 211 81 39

ISBN 84-8185-029-2 (complete collection)
ISBN 84-8185-039-X (volume 01)

Dep. Leg.: B-11.199-1996

Printed in Spain

NEVE ZEDEK PLAZA

Shlomo Aronson

The square at dusk.

Completion date: 1989
Location: Tel Aviv, Israel
Client/Promoter: Tel Aviv Foundation
Collaborators: Judy Green (landscape design), Elisha Rubin (architecture)

In this project, a new dance and theatre centre has been founded in two former school buildings. These have been renovated, and a public square has been created between them. The project forms part of the preservation scheme for the historical XIX-century district of Neve Zedek, the original centre of the modern city of Tel Aviv. Shlomo Aronson (Haifa, 1936) studied landscape architecture in the United States, first at the University of California at Berkeley, and later at Harvard University, Cambridge. He worked for Lawrence Halprin and Associates, and later for the Architects Collaborative, as well as in the Architecture Department in the Greater London Council, and the Department of Engineering in Jerusalem City Council. He set up his own studio in Jerusalem in 1969, with his most important projects all in Israel, including the Mevasseret Zion New Town, the City of David Archaeological Area, the Jerusalem Promenades, the City of Eliat Master Plan and the conveyor belt transporting potash from the Dead Sea. Neve Zedek Plaza has received Israel's most important award for architecture, the Rechter Award. Aronson has developed the educational side of his work in the Bezalel

Academy in Jerusalem, and has on numerous occasions given lectures and talks in various universities in North America and Germany. Shlomo Aronson's office defines itself as specialising in being unspecialised. They prefer commissions where they can take full responsibility for the entire project from beginning to end, from regional planning to the last details of construction. Most of the schemes undertaken by his office are determined by this philosophy. The scheme's first preliminary action was to remove the road and fence separating the two schools. A square was thus created between the facades of the two historical buildings. These facades are characterised by classic simplicity, typical of the style at the turn of the century at these latitudes, with much attention paid to proportion and detail. The most important design decision was to divide this main 30 x 70-m plaza into three sub-areas. The stone-paved central area is situated between the buildings, the entrances to which are flanked by two tall date palms. The other two areas consist of lemon groves defining the borders of the central park. The drainage channels of the lemon trees are laid out and interconnected to form a system of blue ceramic channels inset into the paving stones. The lemon trees form a continuous green crown broken only by the entrances to the square from the outside, marked by four date palms. There is a difference in level across the square which is corrected by two flights of steps providing access to the buildings. The steps leading to the dance centre are semicircular, allowing them to be used for small open air performances and classes. Life is added to tjhe square by the restaurant's terrace spread out over the pavement along one side, and frequented by the regular theatre-goers.

Detail of the ceramic drainage.

Detail of drainage and water channels.

Detail of the water channels.

Aerial view of the paved square.

Aerial view of the location.

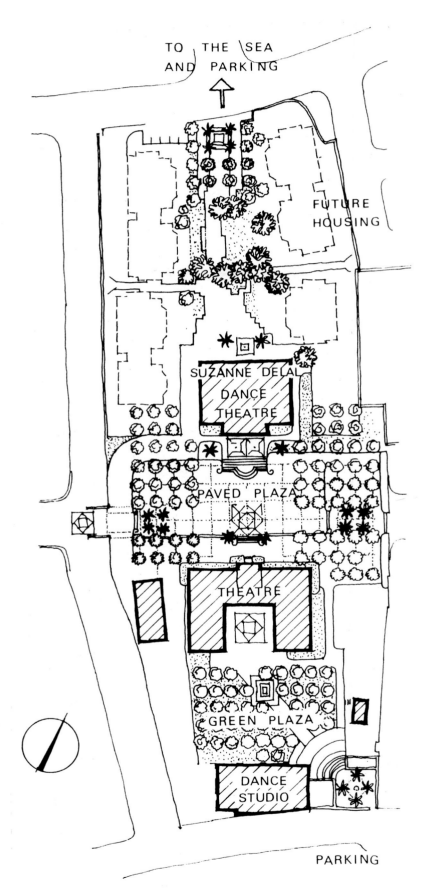

TO THE SEA
AND PARKING

FUTURE HOUSING

SUZANNE DELAL
DANCE
THEATRE

PAVED PLAZA

THEATRE

GREEN PLAZA

DANCE
STUDIO

PARKING

Citrus trees have been planted on grass behind the theatre building, thus creating a secondary square. While work was being carried out on the construction and gardens, an old well was discovered. It was decided to preserve it, and a stone-paved path was built diagonally across the plantation, passing by the restored well and ending at a large old eucalyptus tree. The scheme thus provides a set of outdoor spaces differing in size and use, making them particularly suitable for theatrical event and perfomances. Lemon trees were chosen as the site was originally surrounded by lemon groves.

A triptych depicting the site's founding fathers and the ups and downs of the neighbourhood has been built in ceramic tiles along the side wall of one of the building bordering th space. Apart from showing the history of the surroundings, the ceramic tiles add life and colour to the square.

Neve Zedek Plaza takes on a special character at dusk. The drama of the location has been accentuated by a system of surface illumination which highlights and emphasises the environmental design of the square. The facades of the buildings are lit up by beams of light from the flower-beds. Light recesses in the stone railings light up the space, and the lemon trees are uplit from their water channels to provide relected light in their surroundings, enhancing the natural rhythm of the groves. The groups of palm trees marking the entrances are complemented by pairs of lamp posts in a delicate style reminiscent of the nineteenth century. They are set in stone-sculpted curls inspired by existing plaster motifs flanking the entrance to the theatre, at the end of the stone railing running through the square.

The success of Aronson's project for Neve Zedek Plaza lies in the simplicity and clarity of its spatial design, the ambience and coolness of the channelled water, and the shade of the citrus trees, all adding to the feeling of oasis near the centre of modern Tel Aviv.

Plan of the area.

Site plan.

The citrus trees planted in grass.

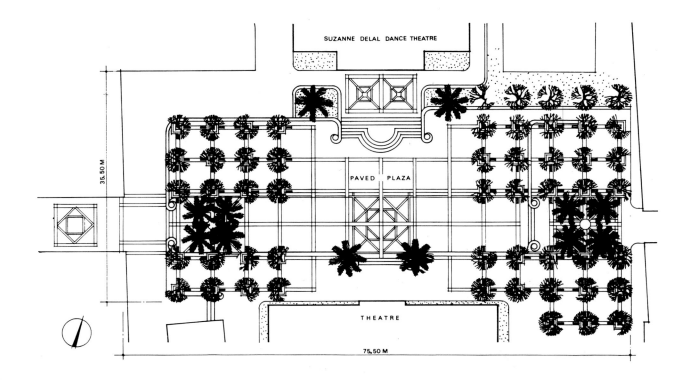

Aerial view of the paved square.

Detail of the ceramic drainage.

View of the theatre building at dusk.

IBM SOLANA

Peter Walker, William Johnson and Partners

Completion date: 1987

Location: Westlake and Southlake, Dallas, Texas (USA)

Client/Promoter: IBM Corporation and the Maguire Thomas Partnership

Collaborators: Ricardo Legorreta Arquitectos, Mitchell/Giurgola Architects; Leason Pomeroy and Associates and Harwood K. Smith & Partners (planning); Carter and Burgess, Inc. (engineering).

The decisive role of landscaping in linking architecture to its environment is one of the keys to understanding this fascinating creative discipline. This design by Peter Walker and his team shows how it is possible to reduce the environmental impact of a large-scale construction and preserve the site's landscape identity. This has also been helped by the contributions of the architects involved in planning this large complex which houses a wide range of functions, including recreational, commercial and administrative areas. The large site chosen for this ambitious project covers 850 acres in Texas, a few miles northwest of the Fort Worth-Dallas airport. The landscape is generally agricultural and rural with pastures and gently rolling hills. Walker's team had to integrate the architecture with its surroundings, and also plan the parking lots and the communication infrastructures. It was decided that the buildings should be no more than five stories high,

Geometry dominates the formal design of the Arrivals Garden.

Small stucco walls by the flowing water.

One of the circular fountains, with mist generators.

Water, free and controlled, plays a strategic role.

Garden-plaza, with an attractive geometric design.

Organic and geometric forms in the corporate sector.

and that, where possible, parking should be sited near the built modules to reduce their impact.

The idea of creative responsibility is often rather disperse in a project that has lasted as long as the Solana project. Until 1990 planning was the responsibility of the Office of Peter Walker and Martha Schwartz, a partnership lasting from 1983 to 1989. Before that, Peter Walker (Pasadena, 1932, and master's degree in Landscape Architecture from the Harvard Graduate School of Design in 1957) had been a partner at Sasaki Walker Associates, consolidating his career with works, mainly in the US. His work at Peter Walker, William Johnson and Partners has become well-known due to projects like this one, which won the 1988 Asla Urban Design and Planning Award, the 1988 Honor Award of the National Prairie Association and the 1990 Asla Design Award.

The masterplan for the Solana site consists of a sequential distribution, starting from the Highway 114 exit ramp, of the three main functional sectors; the residential and recreational area, by Ricardo Legorreta Arquitectos, the marketing centre, by the same company, and the administrative complex and IBM regional headquarters, by Mitchell/Giurgola Architects. Close collaboration between architects, client and landscapers is the reason for the project's success, as it has sought a harmonic equilibrium between aims and results, based on social, economic, aesthetic, cultural and environmental factors.

Respect for the site's natural landscape has been decisive throughout the project, requiring a thorough analysis of the site's topographic, geological, climatic and ecological characteristics and a commitment to conserving the original flora. The natural values of the local landscape were emphasised, maintaining the large wildflower prairies and trees, including post oaks and a few free-standing hickories. The distribution of the buildings and the roads was determined by the existing distribution of vegetation.

Special emphasis is given to the act of entering the complex, showing the importance attached to movement as an essential component of the perception of landscape. Entrance is from the

Architecture and vegetation coexist harmoniously.

highway exit ramp, through the Arrivals Garden, a space that still has a rural feel, although it is highly stylised. Legorreta's architecture encourages this celebration of the concept of entrance, using red Cordovan stucco walls and silent, monolithic, strongly vertical towers in bright colours. Rows of Indian hawthorn, planted like a vineyard, and a regular pool emphasise this sector's horizontal feel.

The recreational and marketing areas develop the idea of a perceptual sequence and the experience of entry. This was done using components like arcades, the vertical towers mentioned above, plazas (especially one acting as a focus for the recreational-residential area) and internal courtyards overlooking the landscape or sculpture gardens.

The radial distribution of modules in the corporate complex favours its integration with its environment. The transition between architecture and natural landscape is in the form of a 900-m-long terraced garden. The coexistence of geometric artificiality and biological forms creates an environment recalling the works of Kandinsky and Miró.

Although water is present throughout the project, in the last sector it is especially important. There is a triangular pool (like those in the neighbouring ranches) flowing into a magnificent

General view of the Arrivals Garden, with the strongly vertical towers in pure tones.

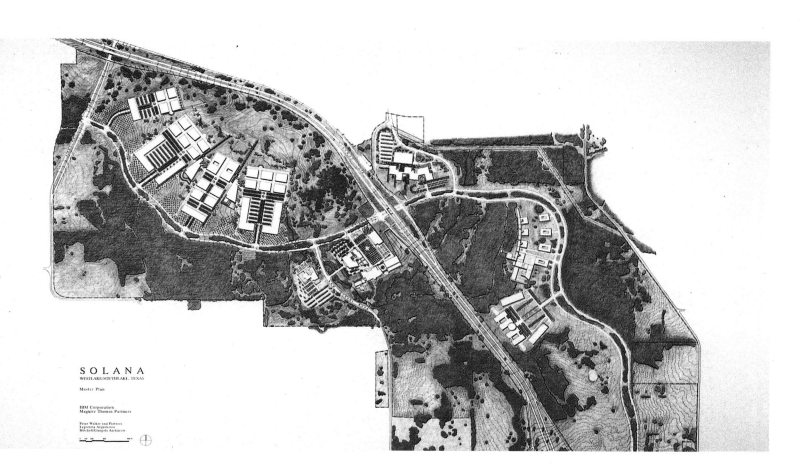

SOLANA
WESTLAKE/SOUTHLAKE, TEXAS

Master Plan

IBM Corporation
Maguire Thomas Partners

Peter Walker and Partners
Legorreta Arquitectos
Mitchell/Giurgola Architects

General plan of the Solana complex.

lake whose design is naturalistic. An important role is also played by water in the fountains, which are very suggestive landscape features. There are three fountains which differ in design, but their strategic use of mist means they all rely on a single cultural and symbolic concept, the contrast between the ancestral values of the native civilisations and new construction technologies. This is the same as the eternal contrast between tradition and the avant-garde.

The functional furnishings encourage rest and contemplation.

The internal spaces are closely linked to the external spaces.

General view of the complex.

The natural prairies, with their lush flowers, have been retained.

LA GARANCE

Atelier Cube

Completion date: 1984

Location: La Garance, CH 1024 Ecublens (Switzerland)

Client/Promoter: William de Rham (De Rham & Cie. SA)

Collaborators: Maurice Pidoux ETS/GPA; Professor Epfl Dr. J. Natterer
and W. Winter, assistant Epfl

In general, sports architecture is associated with the large scale of Olympic events or other very popular sports that require installations with a large capacity. It must not be forgotten that there are other facilities catering for less popular sports requiring more contact with nature. Horse riding is one of the more typical sports in this second group.

This project is an excellent example of how small-scale constructions can resolve basic requirements with greater aesthetic and pragmatic success. The horse-riding facilities at La Garance, in the municipality of Ecublens, are an excellent example of how architecture can fit into the landscape, physically and culturally.

This project was the responsibility of the Lausanne-based company Atelier Cube, one of the most widely recognised companies on the Swiss and European creative panorama. It was founded by Guy Collomb (1950), Marc Collomb (1953) and Patrick Vogel (1952), whose architectural training was basically at the Epfl, the Lausanne Polytechnic, although their horizons have been broadened by studies at other pres-tigious centres,

View of the meadow and some of the competition obstacles.

such as the Cooper Union in New York, or the Zurich Polytechnic (Epfz).

Since 1981, Atelier Cube has performed some of the most important projects completed in the Swiss canton of Vaud, and this has led to widespread recognition and mentions by the jury in the Distinction Vaudoise d'Architecture. One of their first architectural projects made the team famous; their design for the archives of the canton of Vaud received the SIA Prize for Energy, awarded by the Swiss Association of Engineers and Architects, and a special mention from the jury of the Prix Béton 1989, from the Swiss association of manufacturers of cement, lime and gypsum. Their other outstanding projects include a 72-unit dwelling in the rue de la Borde in Lausanne; the prototype modular electrical facility for the Vaud electricity company; the experimental installation in the plasma physics research institute in Ecublens; and the landscaping and improvement of the strip of Voie Suisse by Lake Uri (in collaboration with the architect Ivo Frei).

Another project by Atelier Cube clearly dealing with landscape is the La Garance horse-riding installations in the magnificent Vaud countryside. This context has clearly influenced the project's design and conception. The built facilities are located on a large flat area covering 4 hectares (45,719 m2) alongside

The building is on the edge of the site.

Wood is the main material used throughout.

the river Venoge. There are no access problems as there is a road running through the woodlands.

In terms of landscaping, the project is based on respect for its natural surroundings. This is clearly seen in the emphasis attached to the river Venoge and in the rows of trees running along its banks and those surrounding the large meadow area. This helps to ensure that the irregularly shaped central area is completely isolated from the surrounding areas, which have been affected by the urban growth of Lausanne. Thanks to the presence of the trees, the atmosphere created in the centre is natural and intimate, and this helps the practice of horse riding. The large trees rising over the meadow include oaks, ashes and lindens.

The architectural design has clearly been subordinated to its landscape setting. All the built structures are on the edges of the site, following a design based on longitudinal edges, around which they are grouped. This leaves almost all of the meadow area free. This arrangement distributes all the installations perfectly, including the following competition facilities: jury stand, and public stand for spectators; covered spaces to hold discussions or eat and drink in peace and quiet; a club, studio and housing for the staff. From a sporting point of view, the wooden competition installations are in fixed positions. For some trials, the

Plan showing location of the centre, with the Venoge and the trees around the meadow.

Two elevations of the building, organised into a longitudinal sequence.

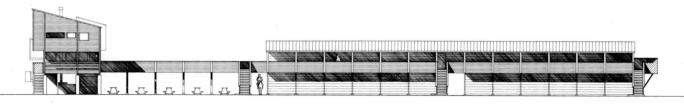

ELEVATION SUD

ELEVATION NORD

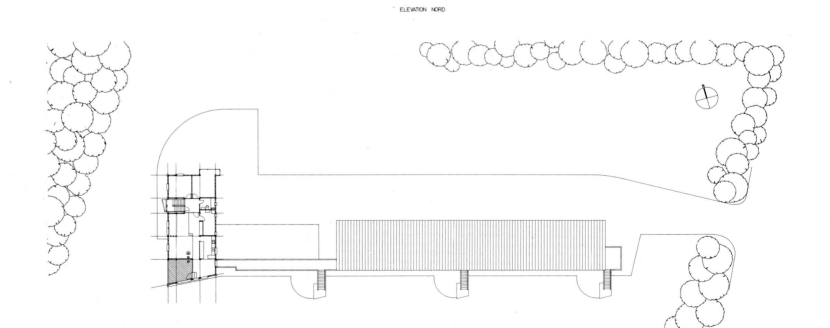

Plan of the second floor of the construction.

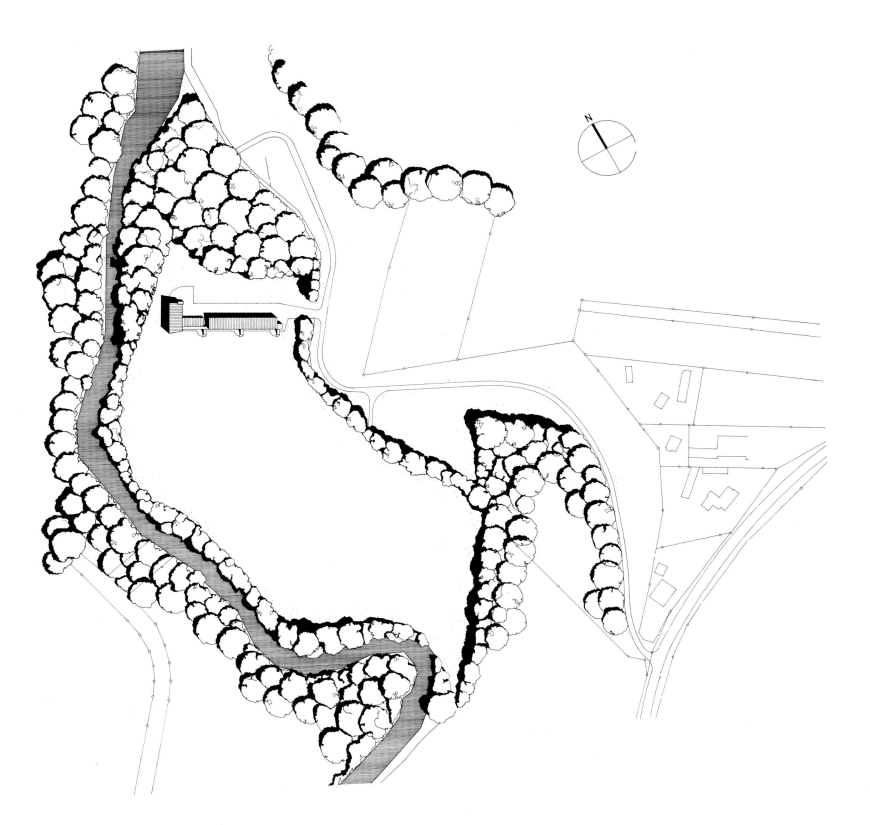

competition circuit is extended, using a curve, beyond the plot towards the only part of the periphery that maintains its rural atmosphere.

The built structures, ie. the competition route, the jury stand and the training area occupy only a small part of the meadow. The rest consists of simple structures with lean-to roofs, sets of large passages and volumes with projecting supports. The pilings and interior staircase are the only non-wooden components.

In fact, the intervention clearly chose to use natural and rural materials, emphasising the use of wood as a distinctive feature. This helps to integrate it into its landscape setting, the idea underlying the entire project. Structurally, a series of cross-shaped pillars, also made of wood, favour the continuity of the attics and the prefabricated panels of the facade.

The final result is one of the best examples of this aspect of sports architecture, fusing together aesthetic beauty and practicality, even though it is more modest than large sports centres and stadia. It also follows a correct feeling for the project's requirement for a natural appearance, making this apparently minor project into one of the most brilliant examples of landscaping applied to the world of sport.

The project is characterised by simple structures.

View of one of the internal dining rooms, connected to the exterior.

View of one of the internal rooms.

Natural light also contributes to the atmosphere inside.

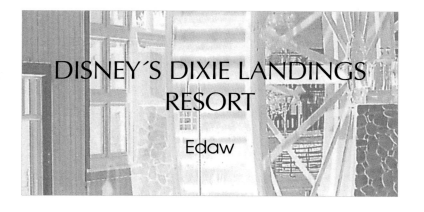

DISNEY'S DIXIE LANDINGS RESORT

Edaw

Completion date: 1992
Location: Orlando, Florida, USA
Client/Promoter: Disney Development Company
Collaborators: Fugleberg Koch Architects

The opening of the new holiday resort for the visitors to the Walt Disney World is an excellent excuse to discuss the work of EDAW, one of the most important firms in landscaping in the second half of the XX century. Its broad, expert and professional team is responsible for this remarkable recreation of the spirit of the deep south, divided into three residential and recreational areas that create an idyllic image of America's recent past.

The EDAW company consists of about 250 professionals, and its name corresponds to the initials of the company's first four members; Eckbo, Dean, Austin and Williams. Now, the company managed by Joseph Brown, Christopher Degenhardt, and Steve Quiggle has many branches throughout Europe, Australia and the Americas. Over the last 20 years the company has received more than 120 awards at local, state and national levels.

Just as its working philosophy is based on control of all the aspects of the creative process, its field of action includes almost all the activities related to landscape architecture and town planning. To select some of their many projects is difficult and fruitless. It is enough to mention such representative works of

One of the constructions in the Village Center.

modern landscaping as the Asia and Pacific Trade Center in Osaka, the Monumental Core of Washington, the Denver Botanic Gardens and the monument in the volcanic area of Mount St. Herlens to see the privileged role EDAW occupies in the contemporary creative panorama.

Together with Joseph Brown, those in charge of the Disney's Dixie landings scheme were Dennis Carmichael and Todd Hill. The design of this large holiday resort, with 3,000 hotel places, shows a theming based on the spirit of the south. This is achieved by organising the space into three residential units, each with a special character and conceptually, formally and aesthetically united by connection to the deep south.

These three groups are: Port Orleans, a representation of a typical district of the city of New Orleans; Magnolia Bend, a recreation of the plantations of the old south; and Alligator Bayou, an evocation of the architecture and landscape of the Louisiana swamps. these three hotel units, each with about 1,000 places, are articulated along an artificial river, the Sassagoula River, that focuses and separates these sectors.

To represent the legendary city of New Orleans, EDAW chose a conception that is typically urban, based on the geometric simplification of the public areas. Thus, the layout of streets, plazas, gardens and promenades is based on urban designs with a simple, rational geometry. The parking areas are located on the perimeter and all the interior is paved to encourage pedestrian circulation. The functional furnishings, in wrought iron, also help to recreate the atmosphere of this southern city. The large central plaza includes a 557 m2 pool, featuring sculptural elements to evoke the spirit of the Mardi gras parades, held during carnival.

Friendly alligators recall the parades on Mardi Gras.

A walk between palms in port orleans.

One of the slides formed by the snake in Port Orleands.

The small port for recreational boats.

The winding body of a gigantic serpent creates a series of landscape episodes, such as slides, bridges or cascades.

The second unit of this large complex is Magnolia Bend, whose reference theme is the large plantations of the south before the American Civil War. here, the 1,000 hotel places are distributed between four independent buildings, based on the sumptuous residences that used to dominate the cotton plantations. These hotels, with their simple but elegant ornamentation, have gardens to the front (facing the pedestrian circuit) and to the rear (facing the River Sassagoula). Respect for preexisting vegetation, careful design of gardens, flower beds and fountains, and the paths connecting the four buildings, all go to make this sector one of the most attractive features of the entire resort.

Alligator Bayou's planning was conditioned by the presence of two large cypresses and a pine grove, leading the architects to create or three distinct "Villages" to evoke an image of the Lousiana Bayou. The architectural composition of the small hotels is simple and informal. Its articulating axis consists of a pedestrian route connecting the three "cottages" and joining them to the main promenade along the Sassagoula. Small bridges in a traditional style border the wetland areas, and the subtropical vegetation, with cypresses and riverside plants, contributes to evoking the atmosphere of the old south.

To finish, it is necessary to mention the place that is the recreational centre for the entire complex, Ol' Man Island. By dredging the bed of the Sassagoula River, EDAW created an island covering 1,600 m2, located between Magnolia Bend and Alligator Bayou. Around it, there is a set of recreational installations including a 6,000 square-foot swimming pool, a children's swimming pool, a spa, games areas, bar, terrace and fishing area.

The geometric simplicity of the urban layout is reminiscent of the city of New Orleans.

A bridge crosses the river Sassagoula.

Alligator Bayou recreates the Lousiana wetlands.

From facades of one of the Magnolia Bend hotels.

View of the Ol' Man Island recreation centre.

View of the water installations in Port Orleans.

View of the Ol' Man Island recreation centre.

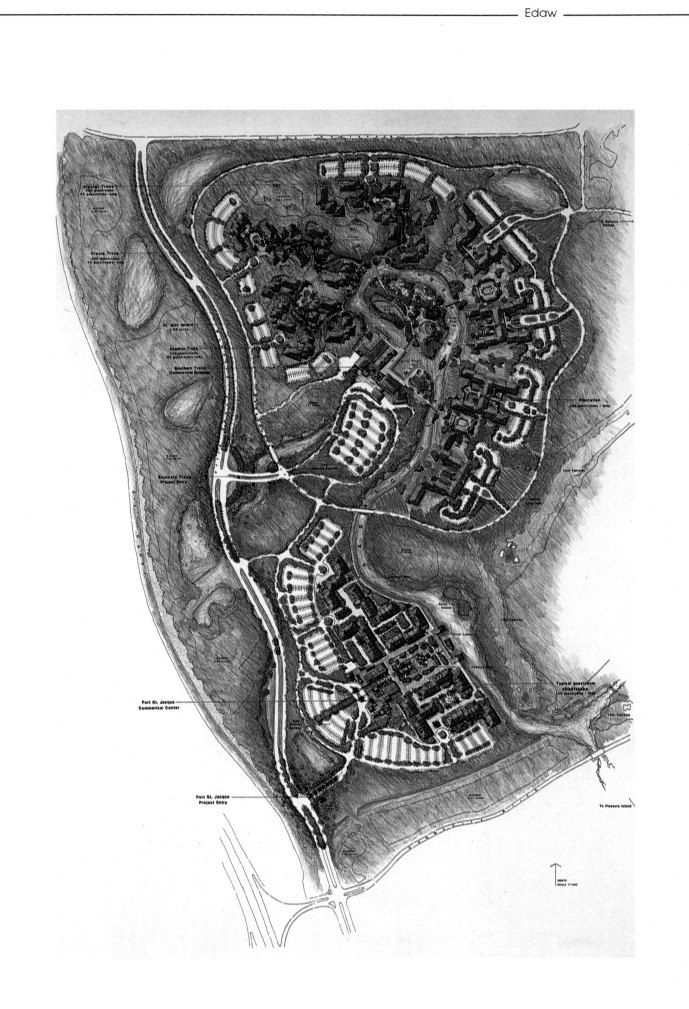

Disney decided on the theme tratment for this resort; a riverside hideaway, with lush, subtropical vegetation recalling a small jungle. The limited range of the original plants, restricted to pines and scrub, made it necessary to plant a variety of plants to create the desired image. Even so, one of the main achievements of the entire shceme was transplanting an almost two-century-old oak that now presides over the centre of the artificial island. Its large size and the immense efforts needed to transplant it emphasise the attraction of this large landscaping scheme by the EDAW group.

The snake at the Mardi Gras Swimming pool in Port Orleans.

The rear facade of the hotels at Magnolia Bend faces the Sassagoula River.

One of the hotels at Alligator Bayou.

GREENPIA TSUNAN

Nikken Sekkei Landscape Design Team

Completion date: 1985

Location: 12300 Akinari, Tsunan-Machi, Nakauonuma-gun, Niijata Prefecture 919-83 (Japan)

Client/Promoter: The Pensin Welfare Service Corporation and the Pensioners' Welfare Promoting Association

Collaborators: Toda Yoshiki Landscape design, Preck Institute, Maeno Nozomi Kenchiku, City Institute & Masahi Muraoka

Although it was conceived essentially as a vacation resort for old people, the functional objetive of the GreenPia Tsunan complex is much broader: to serve as a reflection and scenario of a mature society, in which all three generations, children, adults and the elderly can live together and relate to each other. For this reason, the project of this interdisciplinary company Nikken Sekkei not only influences the wide range of services on offer, but also in the creation of open spaces where health, sport and nature play the leading role.

Covering a total area of 379 ha, the complex seeks to be a recreational space for the central zone of the Japanese archipielago, stretching from the Kanto to the Joetsu-Shinetsu region. The scheme was greatly conditioned, however, by the varied relief and climatic factors. The architects had to subordinate their design to determining factors, like the heavy snowfall (an average snow of 3.2 m) and the variety of features in the heterogeneous landscape.

Aerial view of GreenPia Tsunan.

These initial difficulties turned into incentives, stimulating the imagination and talent of the professionals of Nikken Sekkei, a company that since its foundation in 1950 has become the most important company in the Japanese architectural and engineering panorama. Its interdisciplinary nature means the company is diveded into· several sepcialised groups. The Nikken Sekkei Landscape Design Team takes responsibility for matters directly related to landscaping. This group is structured into three teams, one of which, the Environmental Landscape Group, was directly responsible for the GreenPia Tsunan project.

The wide range of installations, facilities and landscape features required input from specialists from other fields, although general planning and project management were by the Group. Thus, the project was carried out by a wide team of architects, engineers, town planners landscapers, environmental and horticultural experts and designers of sports facilities. This plural system has led to excellent results for the Japanese company, as shown by the awards it has received for works like the Shinjuku Green Tower Building, NEC Corporation Head Office Building and St. Luke´s International Hospital.

Located on the gentle slope of the plain of Mount Naeba, at a height of 650 m, the installations of the GreenPia Tsunan are organised around the nerve centre formed by the hotel-spa, whose multifunctionality responds to the needs of a very varied clientele. The rest of the facilities are radially arranged, following a scheme that makes best use of their connection to the surroundings. These include tennis courts, playing fields, cycle routes, a pony ranch, camping area, ski slopes, a miniature golf course and even an open-air stage.

Stones are used to create natural scenes.

The flowing water connects the different areas of the large central garden.

The trees had to be tall to withstand the rigourous winters.

Even so, one fo the precinct´s most representative spaces is the 5-ha central gardens. Intended as an area for strolling, resting and contemplation, its structure is based on the presence of seven waterfalls, each with a different treatment, and on the streams connecting them. The water used is agricultural and, after passing through the complex, it is returned to its original use. The water is circulated by two submersible 11-kw pumps, disconnected in the winter because the accumulated snow makes it flow naturally. The importance of liquid or solid water in the scheme as a whole is emphasised by the presence of a large pool in the hotel´s access square.

With respect to the vegetation, the basic intention was to create a route through the characteristic flora of this region of central Japan. The varied relief and climate was also a decisive factor when it came to establishing the criteria for selecting the plants used. On the one hand, the natural route starts at a mountain ridge, runs through the valley and ends in a wetland area, thus favouring a wide range of vegetation. The very harsh winters made great precautions necessary in planting and maintenance.

This double conditioning led to several alternatives. With regard to the first aspect, the richness of the terrain favours plantings of species as characteristic as the Japanese varieties of

The climate made it necessary to take great care in the selection and maintenance of the plants.

camellia and holly, Daphniphyllum macropodum var. humile and helionopsis orientalis. In the bog area, occupying almost 2,000 m2, the proliferation of reeds that might have prejudiced the growth of the other water plants, such as Menyanthes trifoliata, Nuphar japonicum, Caltha palustris var. nipponica and Lysichiton camtschatcense. With respect to the climate, the rigourous winters made it necessary to select very hardy trees with their lowest brances more than 4 metres above the ground; white birch, zelkova, maple and Sorbus commixta.

The winter climate also decisively influenced the selection of stony materials used to create circulations routes and outside spaces. Four factors have been determining; low water absorption, to avoid freezing damage; good workability; cheapness and local acquisition; and good aesthetic qualities.

Thus, granite was used to define the outside plaza and the interior precint of the hotel. In the landscape design of the external spaces many local stones were used, creating very expressive natural scenes. The main stones used in the fountains and waterfalls are diorite and black granite.

One of the expressive water installactions.

General plan of the GreenPia Tsunan installations.

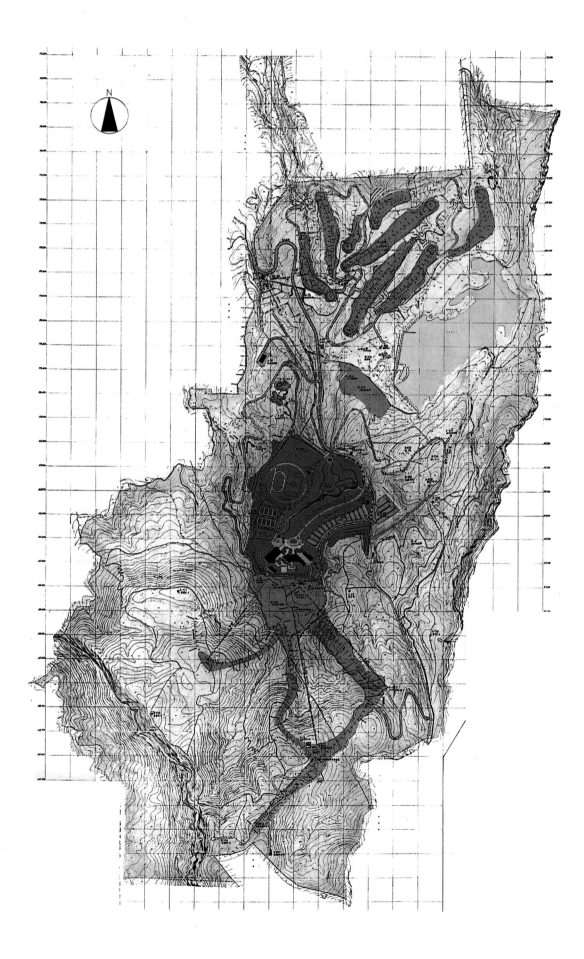

The watercourses also regulate pedestrian traffic.

A winding water feature.

Water plays an aesthetic and playful role.

Aerial view of the GreenPia Tsunan complex covered in snow.

ARCHEON

A. E. van Veen

The built structures are integrated with the landscape.

Completion date: 1994
Location: Alphen aan de Rijn (Holland)
Client/Promoter: Archeon Foundation
Collaborators: Arenthals/Chaudron; Samson-Sijthoff

This article discusses one of the most fascinating recreational landscaping projects, a work based on archeology but reconciling education and entertainment. This park, designed in the beautiful Dutch countryside by the landscaper A. E. van Veen, proposes a magical trip through Dutch history, avoiding the academic severity of museums, by favouring an interesting but educational approach in which contact with nature plays a major role.

Archeon is the fruit of a new concept of museum, inspired by the Archeon Foundation, formed by some of the Netherlands' most prestigious archeologists. Conceived as a theme park, the precinct offers the visitor the opportunity of a physical and cultural trip through the history of the Netherlands, from prehistory (5000 BC) to the beginning of the Dark Ages (500 AD) and including the period of Roman domination. This trip's main attraction is its faithful architectural and landscaping reconstruction of the lifestyles of each of the historical periods represented in Archeon.

The archeological and cultural aspect, conceived and advised by the foundation promoting the park, cannot be separated

from A. E. van Veen's creation of the external spaces of Archeon. She graduated in 1983 from the Professional School of Landscaping and has specialised in the design and maintenance of recreational spaces, country estates and natural areas, as well as consultancy and informative activities.

Her professional experience has taken place within a variety of institutions: she was an independent professional for the authorities of South Holland Province, and worked for four years for North Holland Province. She has also founded her own studio in Dordrecht with clients including public companies, several foundations and many architectural firms. As well as the Archeon project, where she is still working on questions of planting and maintenance, A. E. van Veen has recently worked on projects like the Floriade site, the design of several private gardens and a maintenance and conservation plan for a nature reserve.

The project that has brought her international prestige is this theme park, in which, through archeology, culture meets entertainment. Sited in the locality of Alphen aan de Rijn, at the centre of the "conurbation", almost equidistant from Amsterdam, Rotterdam and the coast of the North Sea, Archeon's site occupies an area of about 60 hectares. The best way to understand the characteristics of this remarkable project is to follow the trip through the park. This route begins at the access square, the main building of which was the Dutch Pavilion at the 1992 Universal Exposition in Seville.

The prehistoric period, chronologically the earliest, comes at the start of the tour, and dates back to the period after the last glaciation. This space clearly shows the original relation between human beings and the wild surroundings they had not yet

The staff, appropriately dressed, show the customs of each period.

Frontal view of one of the hunters' dwellings.

View of several prehistoric dwellings.

The landscape is defined down to the smallest detail.

domesticated. The recreation of the life of a hunter in a hostile environment required substantial changes to the site. Its excessive humidity was incompatible with the need for a dry raised area to represent the period better, so large quantities of sand were added and muddy areas were created next to rocky ones. An artificial pool was also constructed to represent the former Bergummer Lake (Begummermeer), as well as a reedbed on the banks of the river.

The reconstruction of the Roman period is basically organised around the watercourses that divide the park. This interprets the structure of the riverside colonies and the trading system of the times. The importance of the landscape has also been reduced in favour of recreating technical and architectural advances, meaning that the vegetation is subordinated to the buildings and restricted to the edges of the area.

The Dark Age reconstruction shows humanity's first attempts

The plantings and the water recreate the Dutch landscape.

One of the dry areas in the prehistoric sector.

to dominate the environment. Overpopulation in the dry areas made it necessary to colonise the wetlands, a process that led to areas of peat favourable for farming. From an architectural point of view, the recreation of community life in the villages and cities is outstanding.

Three basic factors underlie the landscaping treatment; the layout of the paths, the water and the vegetation. The first consists of three types of paths, one for wheeled traffic, two pedestrian routes and a series of secondary routes that provide better access to different areas. The references to water are a perfect reflection of the Dutch people's relationship to the liquid element. During prehistory hunters chose to live in high, dry areas, but with a stream nearby so they could obtain water and food. In Roman times life was organised alongside rivers, while the Dark Ages saw the beginning of their struggle against the water. All the Netherlands' wetland habitats are represented in Archeon, showing this element's fundamental role in the country's life and history.

The vegetation's role in the park, like that of the water, is to serve as a support for different reconstructions: in prehistory, enclosed and uncultivated; in the Roman period, subordinated to architecture; in the Dark Ages, open and cultivated. The plantings use the most characteristic species, like oak, birch, pines and several types of willow. A. E. van Veen's aim is that over time the vegetation should reach a level of ecological maturity that will help to reinforce the accuracy of the different periods recreated.

Plan of the Archeon installations.

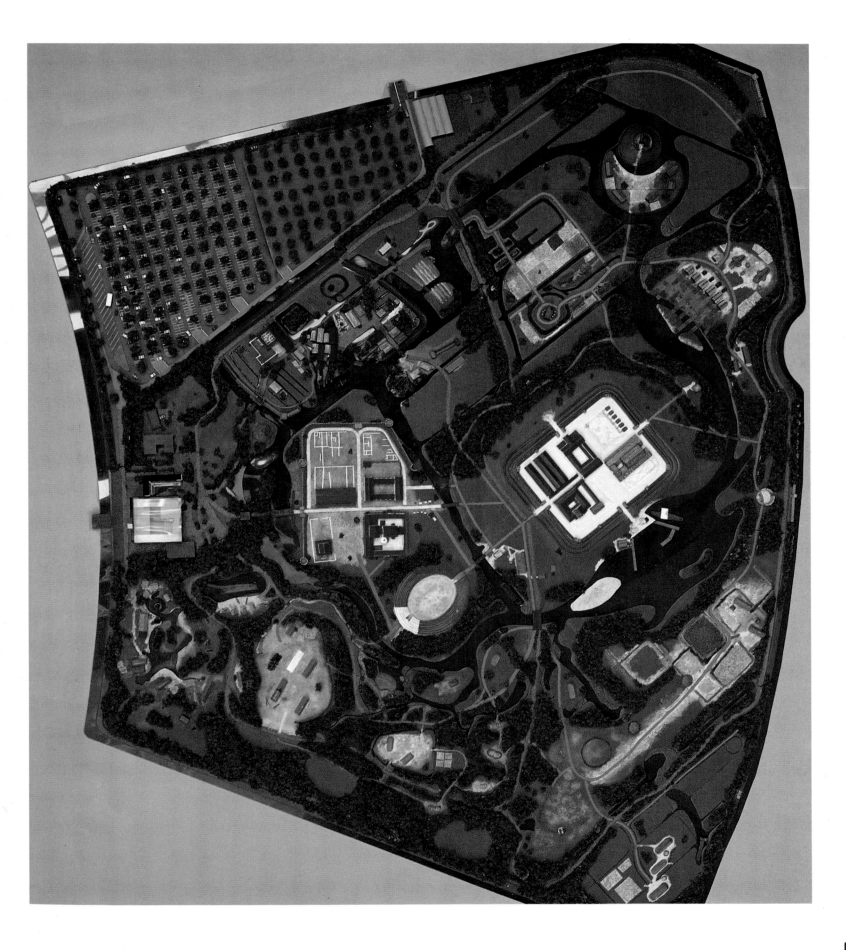

Reconstruction of a small waterfall.

The landscape is defined down to the smallest detail.

EFTELING

Anton Pieck

Completion date: 1950-1994

Location: Kaatsheuvel (Holland)

Client/Promoter: Efteling

Collaborators: Peter Reijnders (technical director); Ton van de Ven
(creative director of landscape design).

This project is different from most of those discussed in this collection. It is not a recent project, a renovation or an extension. Efteling is the result of many years' work and its long history, like the fairy tales it recreates and which are its essence, has run parallel to the history of the Netherlands. Its development process continues today.

The Efteling recreation park has, nevertheless, been included in this volume for a specific reason. In the splendid natural setting of Kaatsheuvel, it is one of the projects which best combines landscaping with recreation. It is no coincidence that it is one of the most popular attractions in Europe (currently almost three million visitors), nor that its merits have led to it winning some of the sector's most prestigious awards. These include the 1972 Pomme d'Or, the highest European honour for recreational tourism, and the 1992 Applause Award, an award for the best amusement park in the world.

Behind this impressive presentation is Anton Pieck, creator of Efteling's conceptual and formal image and one of Holland's

Aerial view of the park.

most charismatic personalities. He has inevitably been compared to Walt Disney, but his originality and autonomous character has made him a unique personality. Anton Pieck was Efteling's designer from the start. Behind Pieck is a person who managed to recreate his imaginative creations on the site: Peter Reijnders is the technical specialist who animates the characters thought up by the artist.

Efteling's history is almost as fascinating as a visit to the park itself. In 1933, two chaplains decided to create a small sports complex with a playgarden for the amusement of children on the site now occupied by the park. Sixteen years passed by before the mayor of Loon op Zand and Kaatsheuvel, R.J.Th. van der Heijden, realised the area's potential as a municipal recreational zone. The space known today as Efteling was first thought of in 1950, and two years later it opened with the aim it still maintains, to be Holland's leading theme park by recreating the best-known European children's stories.

Sleeping Beauty, Longneck, Mother Holle's Well and Snow White were the original four stories represented. There are now 42 stories, although the need to renovate the attractions and adapt them to contemporary tastes has made it necessary to extend the range of facilities to other types of more innovatory attractions. The legendary figures from children's culture currently share the site with the highly innovative recreation facilities. One of Efteling's main attractions is that its traditional aspect is perfectly combined with adaptation to current ideas on leisure.

Since the park was opened in 1952, it has undergone continual growth. Almost every year the number of installations has increased. Some of the most important moments in this develop-

Characters from child mythology appear in the park.

The friendly inhabitants of Laaf.

Little Red Riding Hood is also in Efteling.

There is a magnificent view of the vegetation and water from the Pago-da.

ment are: the inauguration of Queen Fabiola of Belgium's story of the Indian water lilies in 1966; the exciting descent through the rapids of the Piraña, opened in 1983; the Bobsled ride, opened in 1985; the Arabian palace of Fata Morgana, opened in 1986; the Laaf Village, opened in 1990 – this imaginary community now forms part of Dutch culture. Dream Flight – a world of dreams and fairy tales – is one of the most spectacular and attractive achievements of the theme park.

Efteling's development is unstoppable, and another ambitious project is now beginning to take shape next to the park. This is the World of Efteling, with new extensions which will increase the facilities to include other contemporary leisure sectors: an 18-hole golf course (extendable to 27), a new hotel, a recreation centre and a Holiday Village and Bungalows. All this, together with the many services offered (bars, restaurants, shops, conferences, seminars as well as cultural, music and theatre events) makes Efteling one of the most complete and attractive parks on the European continent.

Nevertheless, despite Efteling's wide range of attractions, one should not forget one of its most famous features, its outstanding natural setting. Since it opened, the park's design has been based on respect for its magnificent surroundings. The siting of the installations, the open spaces and the strategic pedestrian path through the park, are all based on the need to give nature the leading role.

Ton van de Ven, the current creative director of landscape design at Efteling, intends to maintain Anton Pieck's original spirit. The large areas of trees, richly varied flower beds, large ponds and stretches of water give Efteling a clearly natural appearance. At times, the park's main attraction is the plantings; 300,000 tulips are planted every year to provide a unique show at the beginning of the tourist season. The plants chosen tend to be subordinated to the theme of the attractions (such as the numerous medicinal herbs around Laaf Village), although this is impossible in some cases (such as Fata Morgana) due to the climate.

Longneck is one of the oldest inhabitants of Efteling.

One of the park's most recent attractions.

The richly varied vegetation provides the setting for the attractions.

Pegasus, a wooden rollercoaster.

The planned entrance to Efteling World.

View at dusk of the Fata Morgana Palace.

PARQUE ESPAÑA

Takenaka Corporation

Aerial view of Parque España in Ise-Shima.

Completion date: 1994

Location: Ise-Shima, Japan

Client/Promoter: Kinki Nippon Railway, Ltd., Villa España de Shima, Ltd.

Collaborators: Peridian (landscaping); Obayashi-Gumi, Kajima, Taisei; Zenidaka-Gumi, Mitsui, Shimizu, Nippon Doken (construction)

The intimate connection between the complex phenomena of architecture and society means that analysis of architecture is inseparable from social concerns. This link is even closer with respect to town planning, the aspect of architecture most closely linked to the social individual, and in constant change as a result of the continuous advancement of the social individual.

This continuous development underlies the capacity to enchant possessed by some schemes, such as the Takenaka Corporation's scheme in Ise-Shima (Mie Prefecture, Japan) to create the Spain theme park. Examining the project's basic features reveals the ideas underlying this Japanese corporation's procedures. The history of this company, now managed by Toichi Takenaka, goes back to 1610 when Tobei Masataka Takenaka started business as a carpenter in Nagoya, initiating what would later be known as the otsumi style. One of his descendants, Toemon Takenaka, registered the company in 1899 in

Kobe, and this was the beginning of a triumphal career that consolidated Takenaka as one of the most substantial names in international architecture.

The commemoration of a historic fact, the arrival in 1549 in Japan of Saint Francis Xavier (a Spanish Jesuit companion of Saint Ignatius of Loyola, born in 1506 and who dedicated his life to the evangelisation of India, Japan and China, where he died in 1552), and the repercussions of this contact of the East with the West are the starting point for this architectural project. There were, however, also economic reasons behind its creation; the intention was to promote tourism in the Ise-Shima area, the site of the most important Shinto shrine in Japan, to attract a greater number of visitors. The similarity of this zone's rugged landscape to the Spanish Costa Brava and the coast of Mallorca also reinforces the choice of the site.

The fusion of commemorative and economic objectives with landscaping conditions the essence of Parque España, which shows architecture's capacity to blur the space-time coordinates that articulate reality, situating itself in a world of wonder and enchantment.

The park's expected three million visitors a year can enjoy a complete vision of Spanish culture and its customs through the different reconstructions in the 113-ha site. This is split into a hotel area with an Andalusian feel (8 ha), a residential area with flats and chalets inspired by those in the Costa del Sol (33 ha), a green space (38 ha) and an amusement park covering 34 hectares.

The design of the park is based on the idea of a tourist route: the visitor is led to excellent miniature reproductions of geograp-

Great care has been taken in the recreation of Andalusian villages, including the wall decorations, the sloping streets, etc.

One of the most frequent features of the recreations of the Spanish rural environment are the fountains.

Typical Andalusian courtyards are reproduced faithfully in the park.

The hotel area within the theme park has an Andalusian feel.

hical or architectural symbols of cities like Madrid, Seville and Barcelona. The visitor can see the Montserrat mountains in the form of a roller coaster, walk through Park Güell and be photographed next to the Cibeles fountain in Madrid. These landscaping symbols were chosen on advice from the Japanese anthropologist and Spanish scholar Yoshio Masuda, who also pointed out the relevance of bringing the visitor into contact with other typical aspects of Spain. These included the gastronomy (represented by fifteen restaurants offering typical food from different regions) and the Spanish character and appearance (about a hundred young Spanish actors from the School of Dramatic Art have been employed to bring the scene to life).

The route through the park's vast area guides the visitor to what may be considered its nerve centre; the reproduction of the Xavier castle (located in Navarre and the birthplace of Saint Francis Xavier). This houses a museum with eleven excellent replicas of Spanish historical and artistic pieces. The circular arrangement of the exhibition rooms prevents crowds and encourages the visitor to discover Spain's prehistory, history and varied geography. It is possible to enjoy the impressive cave paintings of Altamira (an extraordinarily exact reproduction by three Spanish teachers of fine arts) and perfect reproductions of the bell-shaped vase of Ciempozuelos (3000-2000 BC), the Lady of Elche (400-300 BC), the votive crown of the Visigothic King Recesvinto and the cross of Fernando and Sancha (sixth century).

The celebration of the discovery of America is also reproduced in the park; the statue of Columbus and his ship bear witness.

Inside the fabulous reproduction of the Xavier Castle is the park's centre; the museum.

Fountains, reminders of Arabic culture, are symbols of Andalusian architecture.

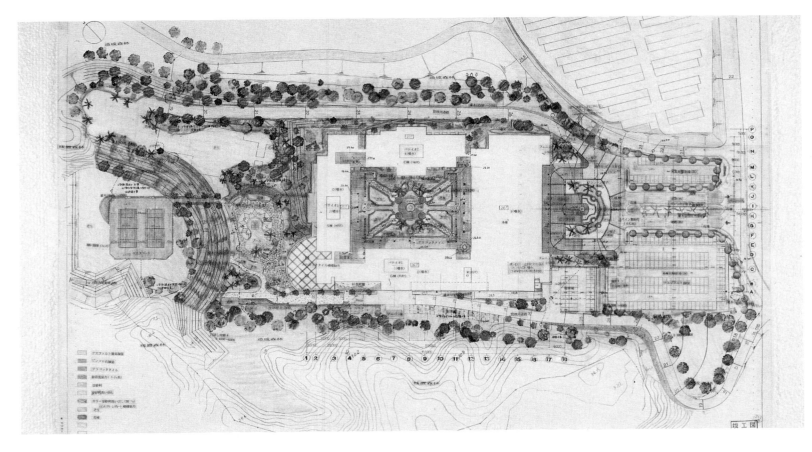

The museum's audiovisual systems also allow the visitor to enjoy the paintings of the great Spanish masters, as well as the native flora and fauna. It is also possible to view some aspects of typical Spanish folklore (regional dress, castanets, etc.) and the process of making some of them, such as wineskins.

As this description shows, Takenaka Corporation has managed to combine different realities to create a harmonious microcosmos that blurs space and time, allowing the concept of the universal to enter.

General Plan.

Location and situation of Parque España.

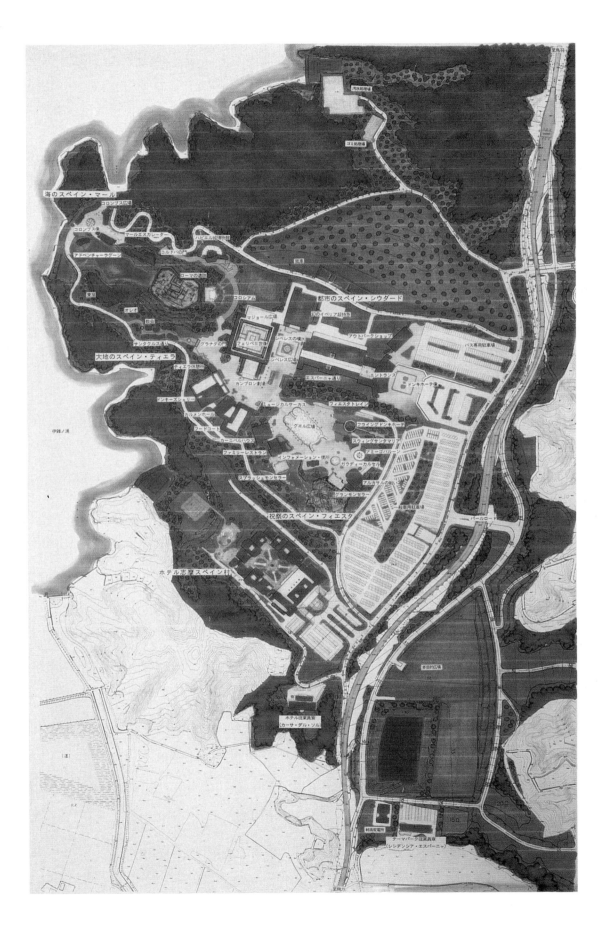

Replica of a typical Andalusian hermitage.

Night falls over the monument to Columbus.

Don Quixote and Sancho Panza are symbols of Spanish idiosyncrasies.

Strategic lighting lessens the formal impact of the fairground.

GENERAL HITCHCOCK HIGHWAY

Joanne Gallaher and Sarah Davis

Completion date: 1989 (end of first phase), 1992-94 (phases 2-3); phase 4 is ongoing

Location: Tucson, Arizona, USA

Client/Promoter: Federal Highway Administration (FHA)

Collaborators: Sarah Davis (forest landscape architect, Coronado National Forest); Mark Taylor (design engineer, FHA); Ben Torres (construction engineer, FHA); Bob Cummings (geotechnical engineer, Engineers International); John Yenter and Jeff Franklin (blasting consultants); Mountain Gravel Construction Company (suppliers)

After the works (April, 1992) reforestation returned the landscape to its natural appearance.

Since Alberti, paintings have been considered as open windows on the real world. But the pictorial representation shown is something more than a replica of the world; the painted landscape is an ordered and rationalised universe. It may be said to be an image of the real world, but it is also the result of a process of formal composition and logical organisation. It was in Italy in the xvii century that the vedutisti school (literally, painters of views) specialised in this type of scene, creating a genuine artistic genre. These painters have been correctly considered as the forerunners of travel postcards, but their great contribution was to show the idea of landscape as a heritage.

*The same point, after widening, showing the deliberate irregularity of the
cuts on the rock's outline.*

Since the beginnings of picturesque landscaping, relations between development and surroundings, and the very notion of landscape, have maintained a dialectical tension of great relevance to the current debate about environmental vulnerability and conservation. This increasing tension has weakened the dominant position that nature traditionally maintained over culture, reversing the roles until nature came to be considered more as a good than as a force. The scarcity this implies makes it urgent to protect, if not restore, our natural heritage, constantly damaged by civilisation's search for progress and expansion.

We could trace a long path through social history from the awakening of ecological awareness to recent incidents that places cultural or artistic values on the same level as natural values. What else can it mean when the German Joseph Beuys – to cite a single example – performs "actions" like planting 6,000 oak trees during the Documenta of Kassel in 1982? It is relevant to note that two years before, Beuys had stood for the European Parliament on the list of the Green Party. In spite of their inevitable contradictions, these demands are usually lamentations due to the impossibility of finding virgin landscapes. In the chance encounter in the Tokyo Tower between Wim Wenders and Werner Herzog in Wender's filmed diary Tokyo-Ga, Herzog says he

Image before widening, showing the rocky slope lacking vegetation and the impact of the protective barrier.

The highway after the first phase of the project was finished, with the city of Tucson in the background.

View of the highway from a residential area.

wants to travel far from this planet to find untouched landscapes, and film uncontaminated images.

Like Wender's career, our voyage from Europe and the first landscape painters takes us to the photogenic scenery of the American deserts, specifically the Sonora desert. It is here that Joanne Gallaher, in collaboration with Sarah Davis (forest landscape architect, Coronado National Forest), is carrying out a project to preserve the landscape from the "scars" caused by widening a highway through the desert. She graduated in Landscape Architecture from Mississippi State University in 1976, and obtained her master's in planning from the University of Minnesota in 1983. Since 1986 Joanne Gallaher has been principal of Wheat-Gallaher & Associates, Inc., and since 1985 she has been landscape architect to the corporation responsible for managing the Coronado National Forest (CNF). Her studio has carried out several schemes for open spaces, and she drew up the design guidelines for environmental treatment of state highways crossing National Forest land in Arizona. As landscaper for the CNF she has participated in a range of schemes; coordination, project management and supervision, slope treatments and levellings, reforestation schemes, designing rest and picnic areas, parking areas, etc. and her work has won many awards.

Partial view before widening.

The General Hitchcock Highway is a Scenic Highway, a picturesque route, with such a stunning landscape that its visual interest exceeds the mere functional need to connect two points. It connects Tucson (Arizona) to the peaks of the Catalina Mountains, and in a mere 25 miles (40 km) it crosses eight plant zones, from the subdesert climate of the Sonora at an altitude of 685 m, to the subalpine forest at 2,700 m (so there is a considerable difference in height). The Catalina Mountains are favourites of American rock climbers and skiers, who use the road for access. In order to reduce maintenance costs it was decided to widen the road, increasing it from 22 ft (about 7 m) to a total constant width of 36 ft (about 11 m), including paved shoulders and gravel foreslopes. Gallaher's commission was to restore the natural appearance of the roadside area within three years of the widening. It had to adjust to a limited budget, a "no-maintenance" condition on establishment of vegetation (which had to be planted within six months) and protection of the background view of the Catalinas from Tucson.

This was carried out with the civil engineers (Federal Highway Administration), by establishing step-by-step criteria to minimise the works' visual impact. One of the main decisions was to elimi-

The distribution of plants follows naturalistic criteria.

Example of the recovery of the roadside.

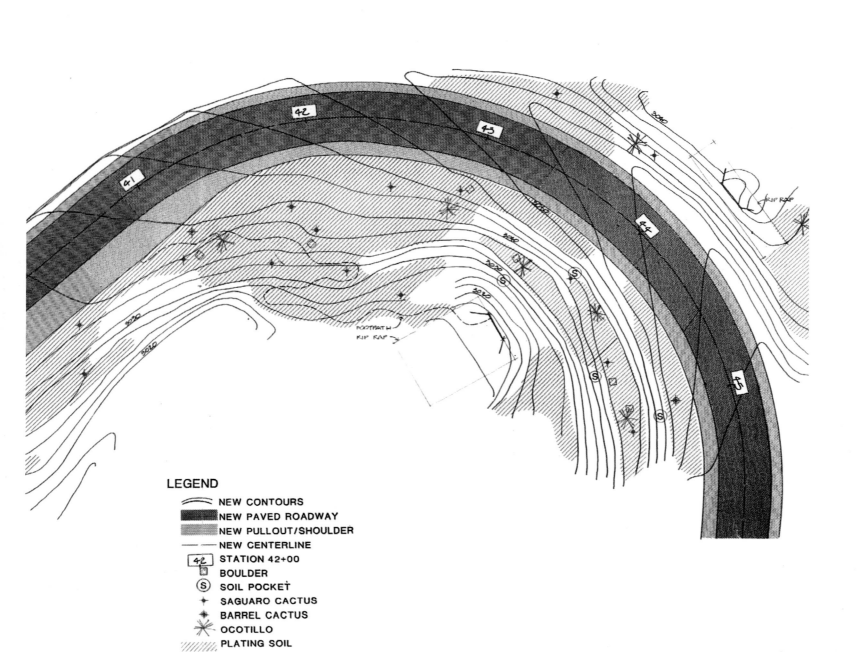

LEGEND

≈	NEW CONTOURS
■	NEW PAVED ROADWAY
▨	NEW PULLOUT/SHOULDER
— —	NEW CENTERLINE
[42]	STATION 42+00
▣	BOULDER
Ⓢ	SOIL POCKET
✛	SAGUARO CACTUS
✦	BARREL CACTUS
✳	OCOTILLO
▨	PLATING SOIL

nate the "sidecasting" of waste materials and the earth left over from the levelling. To do this, reserve areas were created in the points of less background visibility, preferably on the inner edge of the road, saving the unspoilt panoramic view. "Visual priorities" were defined in an inventory of the route's important points drawn up as a working instrument. Assistance from the geologist helped to establish points where it was possible to use natural rock formations, controlling the blasting to create an irregular cut face, with no traces of drill holes, etc. The scheme redistributes the complex former natural landscape, and includes careful replanting of salvaged cacti and the apparently random growth of the bushes, as well as ensuring planting was in line with the site timetable.

Partial plan of the highway with transplanted vegetation.

The same point after widening.

A local cactus is transplanted with great care.

All plants used are native and flowers once more cover the roadside.

Ground-level view of hihway with roadside vegetation.

SHIROTORI GARDEN

Motoo Yoshimura

Completion date: 1990

Location: Nagoya (Japan)

Client/Promoter: City of Nagoya

Collaborators: Masao Nakamura (Sei-u-tei Tea House)

Occasionally, landscaping transcends its academic values and reaches artistic domains that are almost spiritual. This is the intention underlying the design of the Shirotori Garden in Nagoya, a project in which the Japanese architect Motoo Yoshimura confirms his capacity to transform and integrate the three-dimensional components of architecture and nature into a serene, elegant landscape, rather reminiscent of traditional oriental illustrations.

The park's design is a response to the desire to create a place with cultural and historical overtones, set in a natural area that constitutes a compendium of the landscape features typical of this Japanese region. Water, a key theme in the traditional Japanese style, plays a very important role. On this basis, Yoshimura conceived his work as a homage to nature and history, based on a desire to recover the past and to re-store a cultural identity seemingly lost in today's high-tech whirlpool.

Motoo Yoshimura was born in 1937 in the city of Kyoto, and graduated from the city's university in 1965. In 1968 he founded

One of the structures of the Sei-u-tei, the Chouro.

his company, The EDA Co., specialised in landscaping and planning the natural and urban environment. Since 1976 he has published a series of books, already classics, on these activities, and he has lectured on them at Kyoto University of Industrial Arts and Osaka University.

One of the most important points in Yoshimura's career was the design of the Memorial Park for Expo '70 in Osaka, which won him the 1979 Design Award from the Japanese Landscape Society. Since then, his high-quality work has continued to receive great critical and popular acclaim: the Shrine Forest, which won the 1984 Japanese Environmental Agency prize for research and ecological preservation; in 1990 his Tea House won the Uruwashi Architecture Award from Siga Prefecture; and the 1993 Osaka Prefecture's award for the design of the New Umeda City.

Together with these works, the Shirotori Garden is one of the crowning achievements of Yoshimura's career. In 1983 he was invited to participate in the national competition for ideas for the park. In 1991, the jury chose Yoshimura, and the next year he received the Nagoya City Landscape Award. One of the main reasons for this triumph lies in his attitude to his work, more reminiscent of the artist inspired by the site's spirituality than the rational and speculative attitude of the planner.

The park's design was most influenced by references of two types: landscaping and historical. In terms of landscaping, the diversity of the natural episodes typical of the region was symbolically represented in the garden's relief; the mountains of Aichi Prefecture act as a backdrop, accompanied by the waterfalls and streams that descend to the Nobi plain, converging into the River Kiso, which then flows into the Bay of Ise. In terms of historical references, the project's roots delve into the national memory to recover the memory of the three XVI-century warlords who unified the Japanese archipelago.

As a result of these references, the garden's planning was domi-nated by a dramatic and lyrical feel. The gardens occupy four hectares of flat ground on the left bank of the River Horikawa, which runs through the centre of Nagoya. In the face of the

View of the tidal gardens, with the tide going out.

Titanium tube symbolizing shoreline.

rise of high-tech and the stressful rhythm of modern life, the park emphasises the desire to recover and preserve traditional culture, shown by the architectural treatment given to the two main buildings: the Nagoya Congress Centre, in the precinct's northern sector, and the Sei-u-tei Tea House, sited in the interior of the park and the nerve centre for cultural activities in the whole design.

The Tea House is an architectural complex consisting of five structures to hold the tea ceremony and other cultural events, such as haiku (17-syllabe poem) poetry readings and koto recitals. The structure of these buildings is governed by traditional architectural parameters, such as the elegant suikiya style, the close physical and visual relation to the garden, and the typical paper sliding doors. Communication between the different buildings is articulated around a covered corridor that also serves as a functional nexus and sensorial connection to the garden environment. The floor plan also contains symbolic references; it forms the outspread wings of a swan, reflecting the park's name (Shirotori means "white bird"). Work on the installations was by carpenters and craftsmen from Nagoya and Kyoto.

As pointed out above, the natural feature articulating the precinct from a physical and sensory perspective is water, whet-

Stone path around the Kyuko-ken, another structure housing the tea ceremony.

her in the form of streams, ponds or gentle waterfalls. One of the most attractive spaces is the tidal garden, where the tide flows and ebbs, emphasised by the sinuous titanium tube representing the coastline. Another outstanding feature is the small natural sui-kinkutsu (an art form going back to the Edo period) device that produces a dramatic acoustic effect, inspired by the sound of a traditional Japanese instrument, the koto.

Together with the water installations, the park is dotted with a series of pergolas, gazebos and bridges that offer different views of the interior. Uncut local stone is used in the design of the pedestrian routes and in the composition of the landscape scenes. Finally, the wide range of plants, trees and shrubs makes the garden a complete selection of this Japanese region's floral riches.

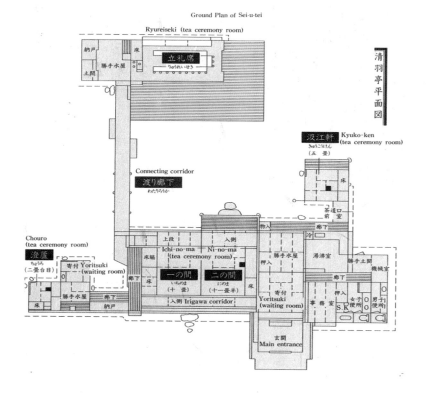

Aerial, almost planimetric, view of the Shirotori Garden.

Floor plan of the different structures of the Sei-u-tei.

The covered communication corridor.

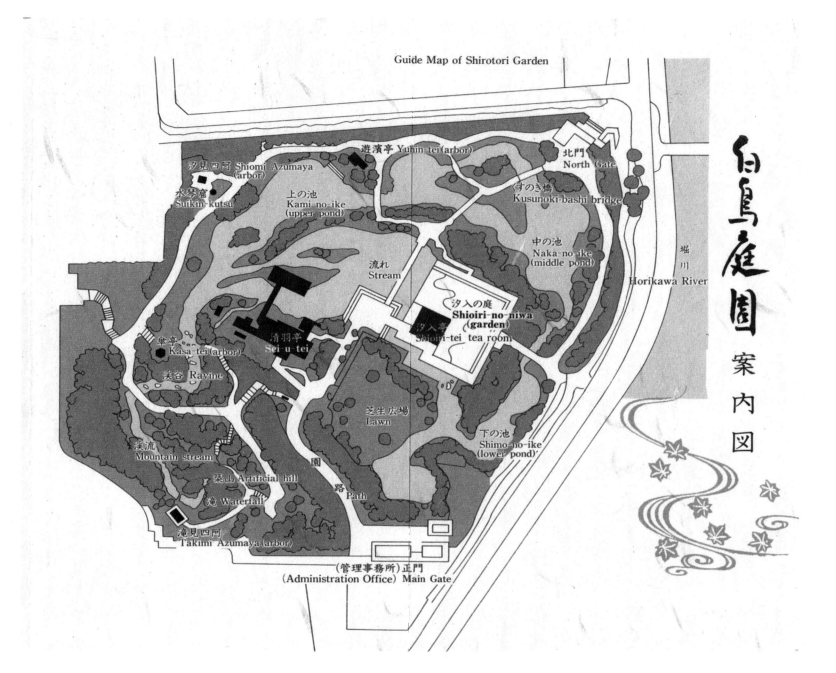

Guide Map of Shirotori Garden

General plan of the Shirotori Garden.

The Kami-no-ike pond and the Yuhin-tei arbor.

View of Sei-u-tei which houses many tea ceremony rooms.

A small gorge that is the bed of one of the watercourses.

The Kami-no-ike pond in the northern part of the park.

CLÀSTICS

Lluís Vilà

Completion Date: 1995

Location: La Garrotxa Volcanic Area Natural Park. Spain.

Lluís Vilà has been conceptually associated with artists like Spoerri and Miralda, because of his use of edible materials such as bread, both to make pictures and in sculptures and installations. Yet this artist belongs to neither the New Realism or kitsch schools. It might be more appropriate to talk of an ironic, reflective look at the world of consumption, like that behind the 1972 creation of the group Tint-1 in Banyoles, which he helped to found.

One of his latest creations is the installation Clàstics in the Croscat volcano in the Garrotxa volcanic zone, at the invitation of the engineers who have remodelled the whole Croscat. It consists of a total of 329 metres of rust-treated metal sheets covering the retaining walls, an interesting 20-metre sculptural group, and a conceptual route made up of icons, foodstuffs and unusual symbolic writings. The ten episodes express the dialogue between people and nature.

On many occasions, rather that merely reflecting imposed requirements, interpretation of the site provides Vilà with the key. It was the sculpture-like geology of the Croscat that inspired him to create this installation, from a site breached repeatedly over

Close-up of the natural sculptural installation.

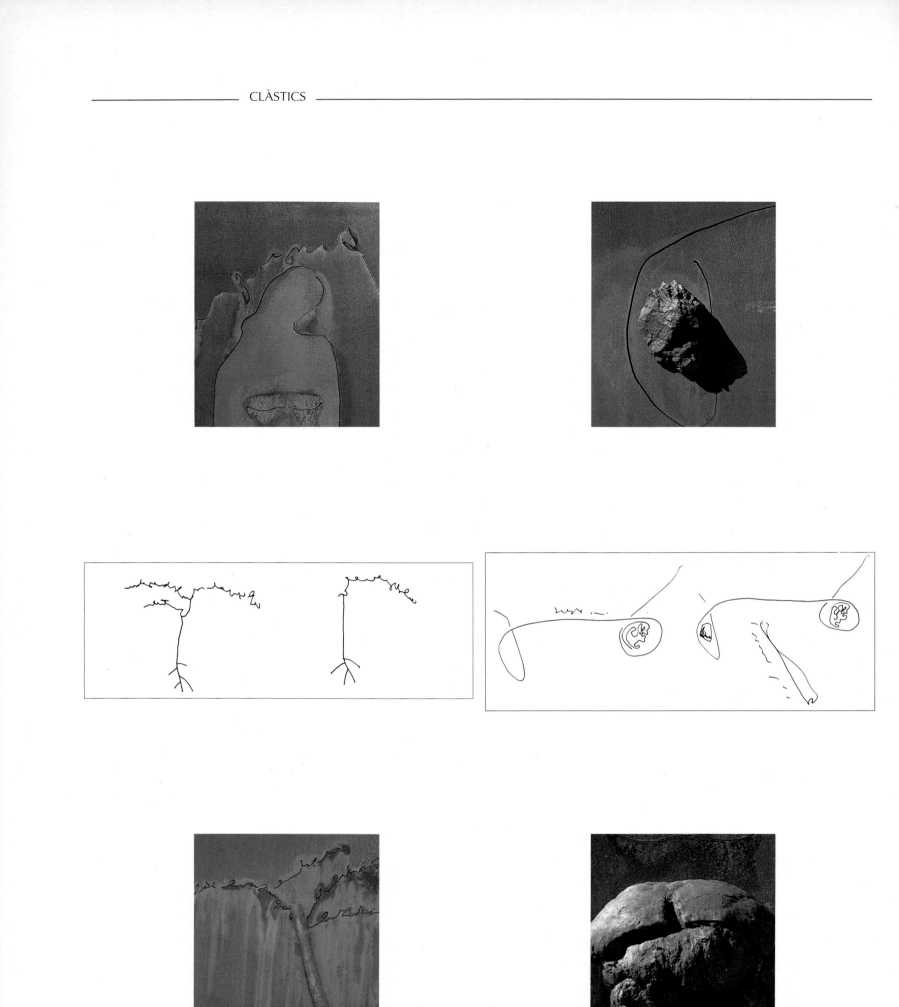

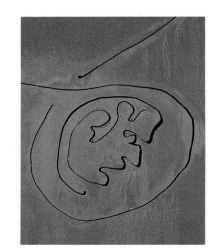

Sequence of illustrations with various fragments of the sculptural installation: tree (tradition); gestation; soul, spirituality; bread (metaphor of time); and microcosm within macrocosm, with scketch.

Lower sketches, visually related with the upper illustrations, show the expressiveness of Vilà's artistic approach.

The restructuring of the Croscat volcano combines geological history, ecology, landscaping and art.

View of the large circular plaza (48 m in diameter), the central feature from which the structural design unfolds.

Vilà's work is a conceptual journey expressing the struggle to reach a balance with nature, and to reach personal and creative harmony by following her example.

the years, as it was exploited as a quarry. The artist says, "This enormous mass is one of the best lessons of sculpture I have ever had. On an energetic level I could feel Nature's vitality in its creativity and in its perfect balance. It makes me think of people's unending struggle for freedom and individual creativity."

Vilà's role was to make a "gesture" in the work's final appearance, but throughout the project he had the opportunity to make suggestions and raise his own artistic opinion on matters relating to proportions, materials and colouring.

The installation's Catalan name, Clàstics, means something formed from fragments ("clastic" in English). This concept underlies the historic and aesthetic design, in which Vilà uses his indecipherable graphics on steel sheets, as if they were blackboards for a "non-reading" from the provisional perspective of human nature. The irony that is such a constant feature of Vilà's work is again abundant. The three strong and highly symbolic features chosen are fossilised by their inclusion in the surface relief of the steel sheets. The bread is a symbol of nature, representing time, the hunger that devours life and consumes all its creations. Stone is the symbol of being, for which Vilà selected some fragments of lava and cast them in steel, meaning that the hand of man reverses the process and returns them to their origin. The third element is the tree, the symbol of absolute reality and tradition – a piece of a cherry tree branch represents the earthly desires, all impatiently awaiting a dialogue to relate them all.

The single conical peak of the Croscat volcano, like Stromboli in outline, is the tallest in the Iberian peninsula at 180 m, and its last eruption (9,500 BC) was the peninsula's most recent. So it combines educational and tourist interest. Geologically, it is well preserved, except for the north and north-west faces. It lies at the heart of the La Garrotxa Volcanic Area Natural Park, which was declared a nature reserve in 1982 for its unusual geology and scientific importance. The restoration project was by agricultural engineers working for the Banyoles company Aspecte, Martirià Figueras (landscaping) and Joan Font (environmental impact assessment).

The sheer size of the cut in the Croscat landscape makes it a "work of art" in its own right. It is not only the support for the artistic creation, but an interactive part of it. Its restoration raised challenges of synthesis and abstraction. The design tried to come up with simultaneous strips of different colours, in order to establish a connection between two essentially different landscapes.

Model showing the section of the volcano that was cut out, and its recovery as an environment combining ecology and tourism.

Aerial view of the La Garrotxa Volcanic Area Natural Park, shortly before completion.

The scheme seeks to reintegrate the volcanic landscape into its wooded agricultural surroundings.

From the central plaza, the topography is stratified into terraces, with drops emphasised by the use of rust-treated sheet metal.

The site's initial relief.

The zone looked like it had been hit by a bomb when the quarrying company left. There was a 25-m-deep spoil heap from the 605 m contour to the 630 m contour. The walls rise from here at an angle of between 75 and 80°, to the 795 m contour line, cutting out a 30° slice that is 180 m deep.

The project's design is based on three types of criteria, geological, ecological and tourism-related, and the scheme is based around two routes. One, green and full of life, seeks to regenerate the site's exterior and merge it into the wooded agricultural landscape. The second route is red and arid, and seeks to preserve and highlight the internal volcanic landscape, emphasising its striking colours and textures and trying to achieve a whole that is suitable for rational use by members of the public.

The scheme modifies the relief by structuring the cut on the basis of a central geometric feature, a circular plaza 48 m in dia-

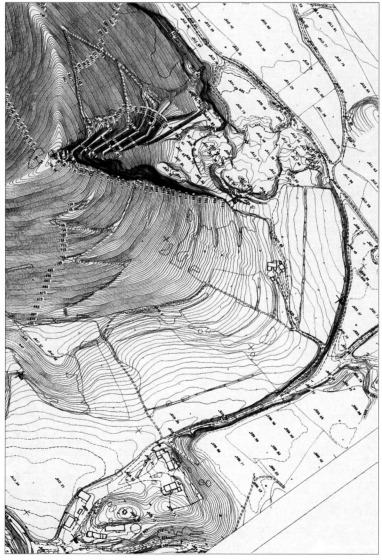

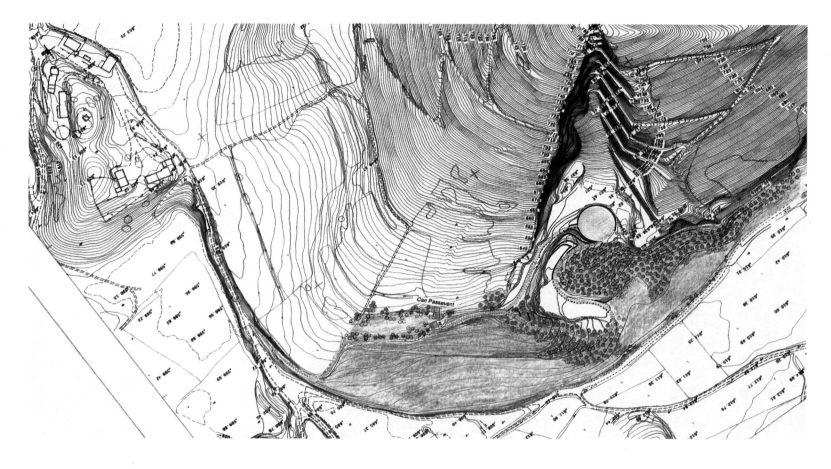

meter. This articulates the whole space, with extensions on both sides in different planes. The steeply rising succession of terraces complete the view from outside by their use of height and vegetation, emphasising the striking landscape of the interior. The use of a set of retaining walls to form a dynamic, stratified structure brings out the plaza's central position. The rust-texture impregnated steel sheets covering the cut of the walls fit in perfectly with the reddish colour of the volcanic gravel.

The scheme suggests a false crater in its very centre, where all the tourism-related aspects are concentrated. The landscape's duality is clearly shown by the curved line the pedestrian route follows. This is more than one kilometre long and the architectural treatment of its materials and textures suggest different feelings and forms of perception.

General project plan.

THE WALL; OAK TREE;
ELM LEAVES; RED POOL;
BALANCED ROCKS...

Andy Goldsworthy

Completion Date: Red Pool: 1995

Oak Tree:1994

Fieldgate:1994

Pound Ridge:1993

Black Stone:1995

Dandelions:1994

Elm Leaves: 1994

Balanced Rocks:1994

Location: Red Pool, Oak Tree, Black Stone, Dandelions, Elm Leaves:
Dumfriesshire.

Pound Ridge: Poundridge.

Balanced Rocks: Mallorca

Direct, unfiltered experience in a world almost completely administered has, by default, been reduced to the realm of childhood. Simultaneous to the global extension of control, now that everything is organised and planned, a generalised, if unspecified, anxiety over the deadening of the sensation of the real has become a background to the frenetic economic activity of world markets. Only in leftover interstitial spaces between regions of economic activity, in wastelands, in enclosed parks, or that tiny mental area subsumed within the system at the very small scale, can direct contact be found with what are now only frag-

Red Pool (Dumfriesshire, 1995).

Pound Ridge. Frontal view.

Oak Tree (Dumfriesshire, 1994). With leaves.

Oak Tree (Dumfriesshire, 1994). Without leaves.

ments of a near extinct pre-capitalist experience.

What remains of that experience, which represented a long period of time when direct collaboration existed between human settlement and the immediate natural surroundings, is the subject matter of much of Andy Goldsworthy's work (Cheshire, United Kingdom, 1956). The shock of direct contact with such real things as the coldness of rain, the heaviness of rock, the coarseness of sand and the gloss and smoothness of material things is now the much reduced domain of children, schizophrenics and artists. As Goldsworthy himself admits, "I need the shock of touch, the resistance of place, materials and weather...."

Working directly with found natural materials, without the prosthetic extension of the tool, the triangular coordinates of eye-hand-mind parallel the circumscribed world of the child's condition, the wonder in small things, the initial orderings of bits of twigs and leaves, and also parallel, more profoundly, human evolution by recalling those first gestures made on a natural organic order by simpler orders of human geometry that prefigured the emergence of writing.

Goldsworthy's weaving of simple patterns and lines with coloured leaves and thorns are superimposed over the very

slowly evolved and deeply complex orders of nature. Each order is clearly recognisable. The lines drawn with leaves along the heavy bough of an oak tree are instantly recognisable as human. The elm leaves strung along a rock dam appear to be the work of a particularly industrious child during a summer afternoon. The dancing line of dandelions tied together on a rock outcrop are instantly distinguishable within the vast undulating moor of Dumfriesshire. Seen from afar, the double loop in The Wall interrupts its original straightness. Black Stone and Red Pool mark points. Recognisable as an early form of writing, the patient and intricate needlework in weaving these leaves into lines is like the labyrinthine intricacy of biblical or Greek storytelling.

This same meandering line, with the patient gathering and hand-selecting, in Goldsworthy's work also refers back to older patterns of human behaviour in the patient cultivation, gathering and selecting of food and materials from the surrounding natural setting. A consciousness of that meandering, but mysterious, continuity is already apparent in the ancient Greek texts of Aeneid.

Any discussion of the labyrinth will find itself turning around the spiny theme of human destiny, and Goldsworthy's work suggests a possible alternative to the present reduction of human activity to the more and more abstract production of information, the

Fieldgate (Poundridge, New York, 1993). Private Collection, New York City. Courtesy of Galerie Lelong.

present condition of estrangement from the real, and a growing amnesia about the past.

The alternative is rooted in Goldsworthy's own English landscape tradition as an alternative to the French tradition, in the continuously evolving old debate between the Gothic and the classical traditions. While it may seem that the debate has long been resolved by the unquestionable victory of classical rationalism and the spirit of human perfectibility over the obscurantist spiritualism of medieval tradition, an evidently growing anxiety suggests serious doubt over the present course of human events. In revealing tiny fragments of a long-past condition Goldsworthy calls into question the whole of subsequent human progress, but, he says, "I am not playing the primitive." His work instead suggests the alternative still possible in the curious scrutiny of the meandering line between two points.

Dandelions (Dumfriesshire, 1994).

Elm Leaves (Dumfriesshire, 1994).

Elm Leaves (Dumfriesshire, 1994).

Balanced Rocks (Mallorca, 1994).

HIMMELSTREPPE
WACHSTUMSSPIRALE

Hansjörg Voth

Himmelstreppe (Marha, Morocco, 1980-1987). The vertical steps rise against the horizon.

Completion date: Himmelstreppe (1980-1987);
Wachstumsspirale (1993-1994)

Location: Himmelstreppe: Marha, Marocco
Wachstumsspirale: Freising- Weihenstephan,
Germany

After definitively settling in Paris, the Romanian sculptor Constantin Brancusi devoted himself to intense creative work. He repeated a fixed repertoire of works, leaving proof of his presence in the photos he took with the box camera that Man Ray gave him. Following these plates, we can see him age and how his studio fills up with works in wood, bronze or alabaster, forcing him into the ever smaller gaps between them. In these years of voluntary reclusion Brancusi was in fact creating his true identity. His figures were repeated in many different versions and demonstrate a solitary labour that transmits the strength and enigma of all myths. The legendary bird, the Maiastra, burns in his hands like a flame, launching not fire but bronze or alabaster to the sky. The Column of the Infinite, which scatters planes of light and shade as if trying to reach the clouds; the staircase that one can go up, but nobody can descend.

Building mirages. Occupying the distance. Giving form to symbols that condense all the tension accumulated on the hori-

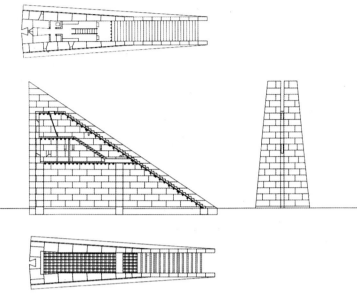

Some sketches for Himmelstreppe.

Above: floor plan, elevation and longitudinal section of Himmelstreppe.

zon into stark but unmistakeable lines. This is the task that Hansjörg Voth has set himself, and it is what connects him to Brancusi. It is difficult to measure and compare these complex works, because in both cases the artistic experience can only be understood as a critical moment. Their works echo down history, becoming as solid as the actual presence of their works.

At the end of the Second World War, Voth (Bad Harzburg, Germany (1940) moved with his family to Bremervörde, where he studied carpentry. He settled in the city-state of Bremen in 1961, where he made friends with students at the local college of art. After travelling to Italy, Morocco, Turkey and Iran, he decided to study painting. He started working independently as an artist in 1968. After collaborating closely with the photographer Ingrid Amslinger since 1963, he married her in 1973.

Between 1980 and 1987 Voth conceived, designed and completed the work Himmelstreppe (Stairway to Heaven), a construction on the desert plain of Marha, in the south of Morocco. He used large blocks of sun-dried clay as the construction material. The work's silhouette is triangular, with a base of 23 m and an upright of 16 metres. Along the 28-m-long hypotenuse, and set in the breadth of the triangle, are the 50 steps that form the stairway. They are flanked by a parapet, 140 cm tall and 52 cm wide, which forms the triangle's surface as it rises above the level of the

The great triangle's front face has a large vertical groove.

111

Himmelstreppe under construction.

steps. The flat surface of the front plate measures 6.80 m at the base and narrows to 3.60 m at the top. This front is broken by a 60-cm-wide groove rising vertically and framing the window holes made from inside.

The single flight of steps leads to a horizontal platform 4 metres below the triangle's apex. From here a stepladder descends to the interior through a hole in the floor and leads to the first internal level. The last stretch of steps follow the same slope as the external stairway and leads to the third and final level, halfway between the base of the triangle and the platform at the summit. It is unnecessary to pass any doors to enter, but one must go up to the platform and descend from there. The act of going up in order to go down into the construction is ritual in nature. As in many other of Voth's experiences, his task did not finish with construction. He then shut himself in it for a few months and planned some additional works, in this case two 3.50 metre wings, installed on a dagger-shaped wooden structure covered with feathers.

Between 1993 and 1994, Hansjörg Voth created another work in Freising-Weihenstephan (Germany) based on one of his recurring themes; the circular arrangement of tree trunks rise like flagpoles and form a landmark visible from far. The Wachstumsspirale (Growth Spiral) is a symbol planted in the landscape, and its circular arrangement opens out like a spiral within a rectangle 55 x 34 m. Its geometric development is determined by nine circumferences, whose radii increase in accordance with the Fibonacci sequence. The 42 trunks are also separated by increasing distances, and they increase in height as the arrangement's horizontal development is emphasised by its incremental vertical growth.

Voth's works are always located in large open spaces, and rise like figures on the horizon, giving form and sharpness to the distant faded silhouette of all mirages.

Himmelstreppe looks like a mirage on the flat desert plain.

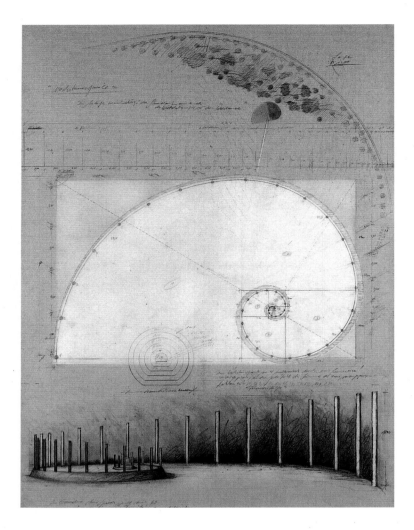

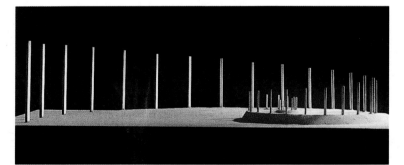

Wachstumsspirale (Freising-Weihen- stephan, Germany, 1993-1994). The base of the installation is its arrangement as a geometric progression.

Scale model of Wachstumsspirale. The tree trunks rise like flagpoles, increasing in height as the geometric progression develops.

The poles of Wachstumsspirale form a symbol of the local territory.

A view of Wachstumsspirale, showing how it creates a sort of internal virtual precinct.

LEONARDO DA VINCI; MARIANNE ; LE DRAPEAU DE L'EUROPE; MESSAGES...

Jacques Simon

Location: The athlete (Saint Florentin, Yonne, 1994)

Leçon de géographie grandeur NATURE (Bretigny, Essonne, 1993)

Hommage à la Neige (Eiffel Tower, 1995)

"Don't touch my land "(Turny, Yonne, 1992)

Burnt Straw (Turny, 1993)

Cheese Land (Chino Airport, California, 1994)

Richesse de L'Avenir (Chailley, 1993)

Burnt Straw in a cornfield (Turny 1993)

Baiser sauvage (Turny, 1993)

"I'm bored without any peasant farmers... signed,   The Land" (Chailley, 1991)

Marianne (Orly Airport, 1989)

Le drapeau de l'Europe (Turny, Yonne, 1990)

Intervention in Cucamonga Creek and iron Wood Canyon (1994)

The athlete in Leonardo da Vinci resists the circle, deforming it with hand and foot; which predominates – the earth or man? Diameter: 180 m (Saint- Florentin, Yonne, August 1994).

The way some artists now defend the reestablishment of contact with nature has been identified on occasions with positions close to the Green movement, a new form of romanticism according to some. In the opinion of those who advance this return to the earth it is essential to overcome several temptations: to evade the clientele of art galleries, resist financial interests,

accept the impermanent nature of their work, relativise their creative activity; in short, to redefine their profession. This is what the practitioners of landscape art have understood, but this does not mean they have not all followed the same path; their paths have varied, and the results have been as different as the different personalities involved.

Jacques Simon has deep ethical commitments. His relationship with nature is highly personal; he modifies it for a few hours, weeks, or even a month, but then he lets it recover its freedom and self-control. Humans do not have the right to control nature permanently. The artist has to abandon the workshop, inquire into nature, replacing canvases with fields, combining biology with aesthetics in fragile ephemeral works that do not disrupt their surroundings. Simon says that the essential character of works of art does not lie in their sale price, their success among the public, their place in history or even in the creative virtues, but in their symbolic value. He defends a conception of art in which everyone can fulfil their creative capacity.

A multi-talented person with deep convictions, Jacques Simon was born in 1930 in Dijon (France). He comes from a rural background, and as a young man worked placing pit props in the open cast iron mines in Kirouna in northern Sweden, and

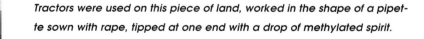

Tractors were used on this piece of land, worked in the shape of a pipette sown with rape, tipped at one end with a drop of methylated spirit.

Fallow field of Phaceha californica, flattened by the artist. Diameter: 190 m (Chailley, Burgundy, June 1994).

Burnt straw (Turny, July 1993).

Sowing of barley near Fontainebleau (1992), waiting for Simon's intervention.

then as a lumberjack in Canada. This was where, in 1955, he performed his first artistic intervention on the landscape, when he painted the trunks of 320 poplars blue, making it look as if the sky had come down to meet the snow-covered earth. After graduating from the École Nationale Supérieure du Paysage de Versailles, he started to condition urban spaces in an attempt to alleviate the disasters committed by some architects in the large cities. He became interested in parks. In 1970 he created the Saint-John-Perse Park in Reims, the point of reference for his later children's parks. After this, his projects started to multiply; motorway service stations, replanning districts of Reims, Nancy, Paris, Beaune. He founded the magazine Espaces Verts (1968-1982), and has collaborated with many other publications, as well as writing many books on landscaping. He now teaches at several schools of architecture and universities in Canada, the United States and France, although he still continues to travel extensively, and now possesses an impressive photographic archive.

Jacques Simon is also the author of ephemeral projects that cast their spell and disappear, projects that aim to please the eye, totally useless in terms of making money but useful to life. Everything begins with an idea, which is followed by texts, sket-

Burnt straw in a cornfield. Length: 48 m (Turny, July 1993).

Cheese land; lucerne cut to form shapes (Chino Airport, California, February 1994).

Simon formed the message "Don't touch my land" by cutting shapes in the lucerne in an 8-ha field (Turny, Yonne, June 1992).

Richesse de l'Avenir; bales made from harvested pea plants (Chailley, 1993).

Double page: shot of the works using water-based paint at Cucamonga Creek and Iron Wood Canyon (Riverside, California, December 1994). Texts by Jacques Simon.

Interplay of the homogeneous and the heterogeneous; of forms and their possible disintegration.

Colour imposes itself to the point of impairing the force of attraction of the nature of the spaces.

The transition from chaos to order is accomplished by means of the recognition of the details that constitute the whole.

The uncertain stability of the composition is what draws the eye to these heaps of rocks.

It is all a question of comfort, forms and tones, coming together to reveal something which may be possible

Colour wrested from chaos, which evokes the way, nomadism.

Colour counteracts repetition in the piles of rocks.

Colours mark boundaries, as if they could not live without each other.

"I'm bored without any peasant farmers.... signed, The Land!" (Chailley, 1991).

One shot of Marianne (Orly Airport, July 1989); 1,200 square metres of petunias, geraniums and cineraria in commemoration of the French Revolution.

Jacques Simon working the land.

Two photographs of the disused factory in Autun (June 1992): two industrial sentinels, the wind and the wires, symbolize an open door to a rainbow-coloured future.

Hommage à la neige (January 6th 1995). At the foot of the Eiffel Tower, the snow covering the Champ de Mars is an invitation to practise grattage.

ches, and finally, in a sort of happening, the idea is made real. Although most of his works are the result of personal undertakings, some, such as Marianne at Orly airport and Le drapeau de l'Europe ("European Flag"), have received institutional support. As part of Le drapeau de l'Europe, the authorities distributed 150,000 two-gram packets of seeds with instructions on how to use them and a message from the Secretary General of the Council of Europe urging people to spread the flag symbolically throughout the continent.

He has, however, acted outside official circuits, too. On March 17th 1991, he erected 52 white crosses on the hard shoulder of the French AI motorway. The action lasted two and a half hours, the time it took the police to arrive and to remove them. He had previously informed the minister by letter that he preferred preventive monuments to commemorative ones. His actions are often spontaneous, such as when he wrote the interjection "Ouf" on the snow at the base of the Eiffel Tower, expressing popular relief at the end of the Gulf War. The term "geographical writing" has often been used to describe Jacques Simon. In many of his interventions, a single phrase in French or English stands out, such as "fallow land = poverty", "Hey! If you have no more forests, you are lost". The materials he uses to emit his poetic and political messages vary greatly. He sometimes uses bales of straw, he burns stubble, he reaps and he uses plaster, as in Henin-Beaumont. On the spoilheaps he wrote "Preserve me", "Resist", "Use me", "I am disappearing". His energy is boundless.

In 1990, Simon received the Premier Grand Prix du Paysage from the French government in recognition of his work as a

Preliminary watercolour for Baiser sauvage.

Baiser sauvage; lips accompanied by a word ("impression") written in straw from a wheatfield (Turny, July 1993).

Leçon de géographie grandeur Nature; drawing of the Earth made in a sprouting wheat field, with strips representing the equator and the polar, temperate, equatorial and desert regions. Diameter: 150 m (Bretigny, Essonne, 1993).

Le drapeau de l'Europe; cornflowers (blue) and marigolds (yellow) flo-
wered from June 16th to July 30th. The seeds were then collected and
distributed, thus symbolically extending the flag (Turny, Yonne, 1990).

Burnt straw in a cornfield. Legth: 48 m (Turny, July 1993).

whole, and for his contribution to the development of a new landscaping language that provides new approaches to the idea of the urban space. He is very active, a tireless rebel against doctrines and dogmas, a countryman, a professor, a landscaper, and an editor as well as being a controversial agitator. Simon does not have the time or the desire to create his own school, but many young willing artists, farmers, and sponsors follow behind him, prepared for every (but not just any) eventuality.

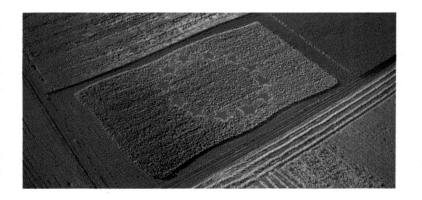

WOODEN BOULDER; BLACK DOME; DIVIDED OAKS

David Nash

Location: Wooden Boulder (Blaenau Ffestiniog)
Black Dome: (Forest of Dean)
Divided Oaks (Blaenau Ffestiniog)
Completion Date: Wooden Boulder, 1980
Black Dome:1986
Divided Oaks:1989

Land artists work where time, material, space and ideas meet. Many have sought to break through art's normal ethical and aesthetic dimensions, widening its field of action, and abandoning its traditional limitations. Technology has made this broadening of horizons possible. Certain ephemeral artistic actions may exist for only a few hours, or they may be intended to develop with the passing of time. Photography and video are thus essential to provide proof of this fleeting moment or continuous development and communicate it. Land art gives art galleries a new role, that of showing slides and films realised in the field.

The notion of duration in time is deeply linked to the work of David Nash. Many of his actions would have been completely lost if they had not been repeatedly photographed. Nevertheless, this British artist is something of a special case, as he retains control of the changes effected on his pieces by time by means of contracts lasting anything up to 30 years.

Wooden Boulder (1980 onwards). Despite its natural appearance it is a rock that can float and bounce in the current.

One of his creative philosophy's most interesting aspects is its observation of the way nature transforms and gradually slowly rubs out the traces of human activity. Nash works on the form of the landscape, taking part in its transformation, and collaborates with nature. Or perhaps it would be better to say they are both at work. His work is alive in two different senses. It is alive because he is working with living organic material, and it is also alive because his creations are never considered to be finished, but evolve and develop as the fruit of his action upon nature.

David Nash was born in 1945 in Esher (Surrey, England). He started by painting and making collages. At this time, his influences were the surrealists Joan Miró and Arshile Gorky, but his interest in material, especially wood, increased. He started using regular sheets from sawmills, then changed to unseasoned wood directly extracted from the tree, and finally to working on the tree itself, whether alive or dead, considered as a volume and

Wooden Boulder (1980 onwards). The flowing waters means the boulder changes position within the watercourse. The different seasons leave their mark on the perpetually-changing work. Like a living organism, it sometimes undergoes phases of dormancy.

structure located in space. According to the artist, he sees each tree as a symbol of life and uniqueness. In Marina Warner's opinion this corresponds to the Cistercian spirit enunciated by Saint Bernard ("No ornamentation, only proportion") and underlies Nash's work, whose spirit shows undeniable affinities with medieval mysticism.

Nash has lived and worked in Blaenau Ffestiniog, North Wales, since 1967. He has transformed a Methodist chapel, Capel Rhiw, into his home and workplace. For him life and work are one. His desire to escape from London was a response to moral principles and economic reasons that led him to seek a simpler life, in line with his ideas. The refurbishment of Capel Rhiw was a decisive undertaking to his later activity.

Near to Blaenau Ffestiniog, in Maentwrog, in a wood covering 4 acres (16,200 m2), Nash performed a sculptural plantation in 1977, called Ash Dome, that was not going to reach maturity until 20 to 30 years after planting. The artist has regularly followed its growth since then. It is a circle of 22 ash trees he has trained to grow sideways and upwards, creating a natural domed precinct. The problem he had to resolve in Ash Dome was to create an outside sculpture with the participation of the elements, rather than struggling against them.

After this work, Nash performed others along the same lines. He has planted many other sculptures, and regularly monitors their growth; each has its own rhythm and makes its mark on its surroundings. Those who have seen them consider them temples built to worship nature. This underlies one of his more recent works, Divided Oaks.

Ash Dome and other works grow continuously, but Wooden Boulder moves continuously. Made from the heartwood of an oak, this wooden "rock" was placed on a slope at the source of a river near Blaenau Ffestiniog, for the current to move. Nash regularly inspects the site as the boulder gradually moves and suffers the effects of the seasons and the climate. It is a living work that progresses even in the artist's absence. It has a life of its own.

In 1986, in the Forest of Dean, Nash erected Black Dome, a 25-foot (7.5 m) circle consisting of pointed, charred larch posts. He arranged them with a rise at the centre to form a shallow dome that will progressively dissolve back into the earth. The wood turns into humus, but the charcoal prevents the appearance of some local plants, so a slight hump will remain, distinguished by slightly different vegetation.

His art became internationally known in the 1980s, and since then he has worked mainly in the United States, Japan, France and the United Kingdom. He now travels the world, from the northern tip of Hokkaido, in Japan, to Tasmania. His aim is to make contact with different landscape repertories; earth, air, water and fire are the elements that appear in his work and for him wood is the fifth element, as it is for the Chinese.

Black Dome (1986 onwards), in the Forest of Dean, is a 25-foot diameter circle in a clearing in the forest. Its appearance varies with the changing seasons.

Black Dome. A detail showing the sharpened points of the larch posts the work consists of. Depending on the season, nature intertwines vegetation.

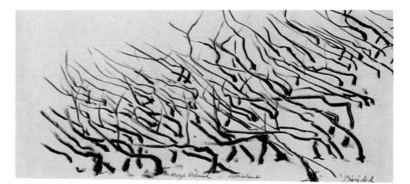

Divided Oaks (1989). Charcoal sketch on paper. Like most of his works, it reaches maturity several decades after planting.

Human action gives the growth of the plantation Divided Oaks its character. Sometimes nature (wind) imposes its direction on the work.

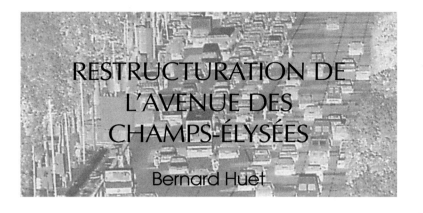

RESTRUCTURATION DE L'AVENUE DES CHAMPS-ÉLYSÉES

Bernard Huet

Completion date: September, 1994

Location: Paris (France)

Client/Promoter: Ville de Paris, Mission Champs-Élysées

Collaborators: Olivier Bressac and Jean-Baptiste Suet (project designers); Omnium Général d'Ingénierie (engineering); Jean-Michel Wilmotte and Marc Dutoit (urban furnishings); Gtm-ds (constructor of the car park)

Just as the silhouette of Notre-Dame and the Eiffel Tower have become fixed in the mind as the popular image of Paris, the Champs-Élysées is also part of unforgettable landscape. Yet this site's identity does not derive from a "central feature" such as a monument, but from the space created by the public thoroughfare. Created by Lenôtre in the xvii century, over the next two centuries it was developed, then reorganised in the style of Haussmann by Alphand, and then extended to the Grande Arche de la Défense, but even so this urban design has maintained its vigour. This has been due to its simplicity and its clear geometry, which has remained unaffected by architectural treatments and time. Without a doubt, the Arc de Triomphe de l'Étoile is a striking focal point in the perspective. However, it is the alignment and size of the architectural structures flanking the avenue, rather than the quality (often modest) of their facades conside-

View along the avenue after the restructuring directed by Bernard Huet.

Various views after the intervention.

red in isolation, that makes this urban composition so coherent. As Bernard Huet points out, in this case the leading role is played by factors like the paving, the alignment of the trees and the design of the urban furnishings.

The construction of car parks and the opening of the side lanes to traffic, followed in the 1950s by the removal of the two external rows of trees, and then the disorderly growth of the urban furnishings and café terraces forced Paris Council to call a competition in 1990 for designs to reconstruct the avenue. This competition was part of a larger plan to upgrade the axis running from the Grand Louvre to Nanterre and St.-Germain, and the "promenade" of the Champs-Élysées forms the most prestigious part of this scheme. Thus the object of the competition was to resurect the original intention of it as a place where people could take a walk. To achieve this, its was necessary to eliminate the 490 parking spaces on streets level and create and underground car park with space for 800 cars underneath the existing trees.

It is difficult to sum up Bernard Huet's career in a few lines, and even more difficult to show his influence on many students and architects, and what his works have given to contemporary design. He has won the Grand Prix de la Critique Architecturale (1983), the Grand Prix de l'Urbanisme et de l'Art Urbain (1993) and the Prix de l'Amenagement Urbain (1994) and has taught in many countries (he was responsible for the creation of UP 8 in Paris, two research institutes – Ierau and Ipraus – and a postgraduate course, CEA). He is also an expert advisor to many commissions and institutions (Unesco, Cnrs, Commission Nationale des Abords des Monuments Historiques, etc.), and has successfully blended theory and practice, a combination that he has always defended with total conviction. The positions he adopted as chief editor of Architecture d'Aujourd'hui between 1974 and 1977 led to his international recognition. Breaking with the modernist tradition that reduced architecture to a "work-object", limiting it to something for specialists, he raised key questions about the function and status of architecture. He also advanced the idea that architecture is for everybody and must respond to social demands, and this means that architecture cannot be practised without a critical and theoretical reflection extending beyond the framework of architecture.

Before any attempt to develop the project, in his professional activity Huet aims for thorough analysis of the site and its past. To decipher the details of history is to understand why one thing was maintained or changed at any given moment; this makes it possible to discover all the factors distorting the original image. In this case, recovering the legibility of the urban project "must of necessity return to the vigorous thought that inspired this great urban composition". Lenôtre's principle, respected by Alphand and Hittorff, was based on the simple repetition of several identical forms (trees and furnishings). To recover this unity and visual order, Bernard Huet's studio used the same concept to generate a permanent interaction between the geometric system of the paving design and the "urban disorder" derived from the different uses of the pavements and the large number of situations needing to be solved; the junctions with the secondary streets, the variable spacing of the trees, leaving the exits to the metro system untouched, as well as the rational organisation of pedestrian circulation, café terraces and urban furnishings.

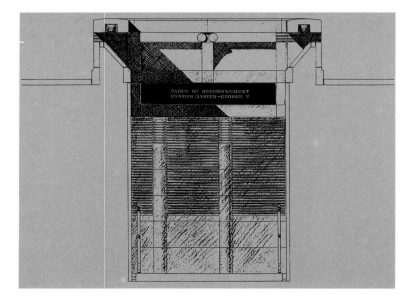

The pavements are all on the same level, requiring the design of an adequate rainfall drainage system, and are arranged into two groups differentiated by their function and the treatment of the ground surface. The pedestrian promenade has been completely cleared except for the exits from the metro and car parks, and has a design based on slabs of light grey granite, dotted with small bluish-grey pavers, masking the anomalies in the alignment of the trees by reinforcing the perspective of the pedestrian route. In the second group of pavements, between the new row of trees and the buildings, the rhythm is marked by small light pavers, crossed by darker series of double lateral strips aligned with the trees. At this point, the design also covers up the slight irregularities in the alignment of the trees and refers to the more static nature of the surrounding buildings, such as bars, boutiques and building entrances.

This system serves as a base for the siting of the urban furnishings. The lampposts created by Hittorff in 1837 and the new features designed by Jean-Michel Wilmotte had to be sited along the axis of the lines of trees, which is given form in light granite that fills the space between the two strips of dark granite. This siting principle and the designers' search for unity of appearan-

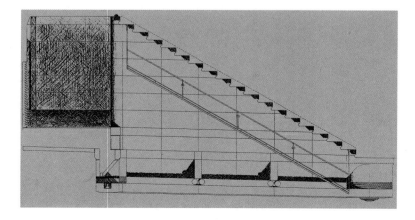

Cross and longitudinal sections of the car park entrance.

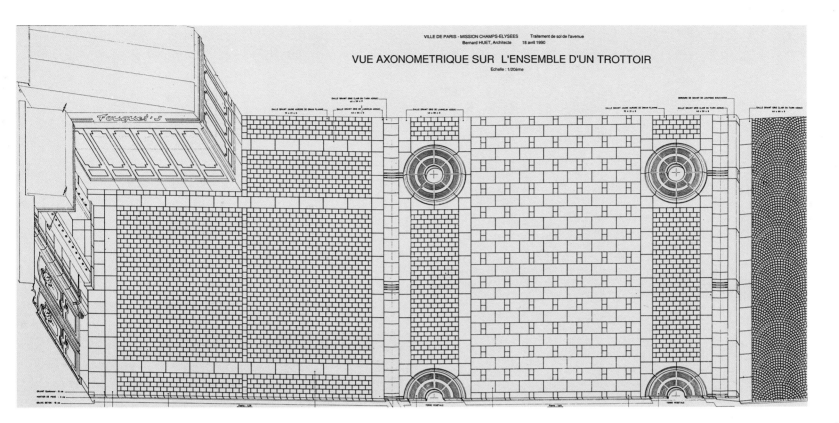

VILLE DE PARIS - MISSION CHAMPS-ELYSEES   Traitement de sol de l'avenue
Bernard HUET, Architecte   18 avril 1990

VUE AXONOMETRIQUE SUR L'ENSEMBLE D'UN TROTTOIR

Echelle : 1/20ème

Typical detail of the geometric and arithmetic system governing the pavement design.

Type plan of a sector of the avenue; the treatment of the ground surfaces is based on distinguishing the zones by their function.

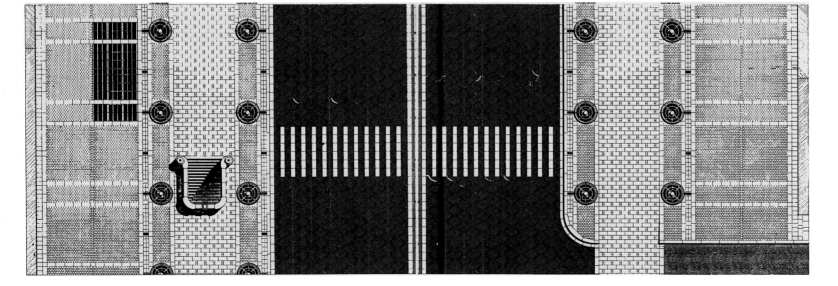

ce, colours and materials was intended to reinforce the spatial perception and coherence of an urban design in which the interventions over the centuries have been the result of a single line of thought.

The interaction between the designs, the granite and the shade cast by the plane trees produces real aesthetic pleasure.

This view show the dual nature of the treatment of the avenue's pedestrian zones.

Detail of the basin around a tree (without the protective grille), surrounded by a small channel connecting to the general drainage system.

POLICE BOX

Koichi Yasuda (Nikken Sekkei Tokyo)

Completion date: 1993

Location: Kokyo-Gaien Chiyoda-ku, Tokyo (Japan)

Client/Promoter: Tokyo Metropolitan Police Board Building Department

Collaborators: Koichi Nakayashiki (architect); Takayuki Teramoto (structural engineer); Koichi Suzuki (electrical engineer); Hiroaki Nagahama (mechanical engineer)

This building is sited next to a bridge leading to the main entrance to the residence of the Japanese imperial family, the Sakuradamon gate to the Edo castle. It shows an admirable combination of two quite distinct scales. One is the intimate scale of the gatekeeper, the patient wait, the actions repeated in front of the office clock, movements inevitably ordered by the second hand. At the opposite end of the scale is the timelessness of the Imperial Palace, its pavilions with their pointed roofs, its ancient trees, its wall protected by the immense calm moat – the scale of our historical heritage and its persistence.

The architect saw the design as an exercise in simplicity, humility and respect for the historic setting, but at the same time it resolves the details by making constant, subtle references to the magnificent surrounding architecture and to nature herself, making the small building into a reflection of these virtues.

The Tokyo Police Department commissioned the design from

View from the moat: photomontage.

the Nikken Sekkei company. Founded in 1950, Nikken Sekkei brings together professionals from different fields within architecture, engineering, town planning and landscaping, and is now one of Japan's main design companies. On this occasion, the multidisciplinary group of collaborators from the company was directed by the architect Koichi Yasuda, winner of the 1981 Tokyo Institute of Technology Best Diploma Project Prize and a former collaborator of Bernard Tschumi in New York. This project won the SD Review Prize in September 1993, which he won again the next year with his project Flying Tube.

The police box to guard the 300-year-old bridge and moat had to be sited on the promenade around the moat, and thus could not exceed the specified size (2.3 m wide and 10 m long), meaning it was about the size of a normal item of urban furniture. Despite its smallness, it had to include an office, toilet facilities, a small kitchen and a rest room with a tatami (traditional Japanese mat).

One of the architect's main design guidelines was a gradient of light, from light to dark, running along the building's longitudi-

Two structural details: graded windows and low walls of stacked glass.

nal axis, and this concept led him to the definition of the external walls and the distribution of the design components. On the west side, overlooking the avenue around the moat and opposite the recently-built skyscraper office blocks running along the passage, the wall consists of a double safety glass (2 x 8 mm) wall with a set of adjustable aluminium sheet louvers inside. There is a gradation in the perforation of the louvers to ensure a gradient of light penetration.

The aluminium louvers behind the glass cause it to reflect the buildings opposite, and the square perforations, which are the size of the reflections of the office block windows, produce an effect blending the reality with the reflection. The effect persists at night, due to the electric lighting inside, filtering through the calculatedly irregular perforations, seemingly as random as the office windows lit when late-night decisions are being taken.

Along the west side there is a narrow corridor lit by the points of light shining through the louver, showing a gradation in light intensity. Here, the gradient of light corresponds to the privacy of the rooms, ranging from darkness in the tatami room to brightness in the small office and porch. This is where the police station fulfils its true purpose – it is a sentry post with an excellent view of the bridge and the first pavilion, like a perfect photographic

View from the promenade.

145

composition.

The toilet facilities, kitchen and wardrobe form a block between the public and the private areas, and are conceived as a wardrobe with three sides. The floor is paved in grey ceramic tiles, the same colour as the paving of the promenade. The square aluminium panels used for the ceiling have a round central light fitting and are perforated to allow better absorption of sound.

The lower part of the eastern wall, the side facing the moat, consists of a wall of stacked 15-mm-thick glass sheets. The direct light shining through them produces the same effect as light shining through water. There is also a further slight continuous rippling effect, caused by the light reflected by the water in the moat. Thus, the floor of the police box shows a splendid private show of constantly moving reflections, as if it was a representation of a pool or river.

The building has a very simple form (four walls and a roof) and a colour (light grey) that avoids being discordant: basically it is a small box, a building the size of a bus stop, rather bigger than a telephone box or the traffic signs on a major avenue. It passes unnoticed next to the spectacular Imperial Palace, surrounded

Two nighttime views.

View from the interior, of the aluminium louvers.

Aerial photo showing the location.

Constructive axonometric projection.

Constructive cross-section.

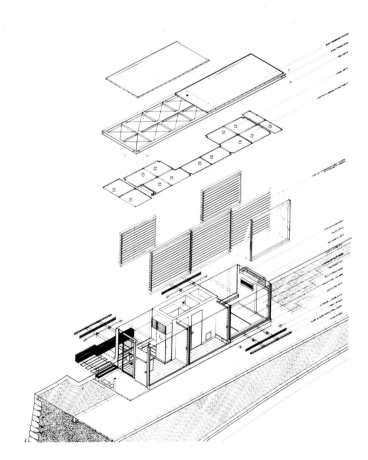

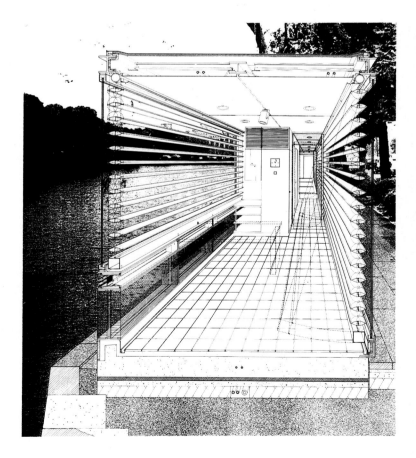

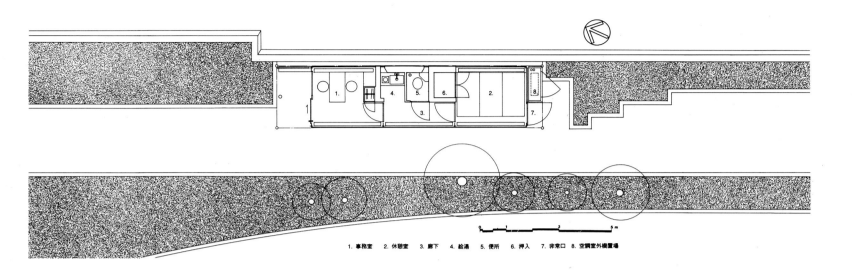

1. 事務室　2. 休憩室　3. 廊下　4. 給湯　5. 便所　6. 押入　7. 非常口　8. 空調室外機置場

Ground plan of the police box.

1. Office

2. Tatami room

3. Corridor

4. Kitchen

5. Toilet

6. Wardrobe

7. Emergency exit

8. Installations

Variations in the west facade at different times.

by huge trees growing over the wall and reflected in the waters of the moat. It could not have been otherwise. It is an act of conscious humility, an awareness full of wisdom. It is full of the same subtlety as those who built the castle on the other side of the moat, based on light, on reflections, on nightfall and the beauty of the sun as it rises through the trees.

This building is always changing, due to the reflections of the water, to the changes in the light from moment to moment... because an observation post is above all a place for waiting, for the personal verification of the passing of time... a time that repeats.

General view from the moat.

Grade windows and low walls of stacked glass.

Interior view of the office.

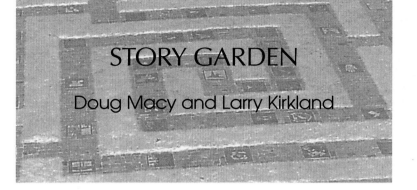

STORY GARDEN

Doug Macy and Larry Kirkland

The maze lies between four points: the throne, the threshold, the hare and the tortoise.

Completion date: 1993

Location: Waterfront Park, Portland, Oregon (USA)

Client/Promoter: City of Portland; funding by Bureau of Parks, Fred Meyer Trust, Portland Development Commission, Burlington Northern Foundation, Thurston Foundation, Portland Gas Company, Davis Wright Tremaine

Collaborators: David Oldfield (child psychologist)

Doug Macy and Larry Kirkland's Story Garden is a unique landscape in Waterfront Park, Portland, Oregon. Fables, myths and reality blend to make a fantastic maze that is a metaphor of life. A surprising environment that entertains the visitors and encourages them to create their own narrative, by raising questions and offering answers.

This work is the result of the collaboration between the landscape architect Doug Macy and the artist Larry Kirkland. J. Douglas Macy studied Landscape Architecture at the University of Oregon (graduating in 1969) and at Oregon State University (1963-1966), and has been working professionally for over 25 years. He is a founding partner of the company Walker & Macy, where he has worked since 1976. Before this he worked with Warner and Walker Associates in 1968 and 1969, and with the

Perron Partnership, P.C. from 1969 to 1976. His production includes the development plan for the Washington Park Zoo Development Plan (Portland), the Vietnam Veterans of Oregon Memorial (Portland), the Metro 2040 Planning Project for Portland and vicinity, and the new installations for Willamette University (Salem, Oregon).

The Story Garden is a two-dimensional maze 60 feet (18.30 m) in diameter, on the lush grass of Waterfront Park. In the center of the maze the path winds around, never ending at a central goal, but entering into granite pathways. Dominating the maze area is a small knoll topped with a massive red granite throne, overlooking the maze. At the opposite end, a stone platform acts as the base for a gate built of tiny geometric pieces, reminiscent of "buildings" made with the pieces of a child's construction set. The perpendicular axis has a granite statue at each of its ends, one representing a tortoise and the other a hare, in clear allusion to the fable. Thus, the four points of the maze are defined by the throne, the gate (or threshold), the tortoise and the hare. Granite cubes, like the ones used to construct the gate, ring the maze's perimeter.

Visitors become participants by walking along the monument.

The throne has an excellent view of the monument.

Aerial view of the monument.

Aerial view: the maze blends in with its fluvial environment.

Along the paths making up the monument are more than a hundred and fifty 16 x 16 in. (40.60 x 40.60 cm) granite pavers with different etched images telling stories like "Jonah and the Whale" and "Little Red Riding Hood". By the threshold are images of the dawn, spring and childhood. By the hare there are scenes of the hot midday, summer and youth. Under the throne the images represent power, adulthood, autumn and dusk. The images near the tortoise refer to wisdom, age, winter and night. The images on the paths show the situations and events that form the milestones in every person's life.

To plan the Story Garden, Macy and Kirkland interviewed child psychologists, parents, policemen, and park and garden maintenance staff. The final form of the monument had to be acceptable to all of them and fulfil the requirements of safety, visibility and accessibility. The Story Garden is not merely a decorative feature, a visual whim. It can be considered as a sort of mental exercise, a simple hieroglyphic full of symbols and representations, a place that is suitable for both leisure and reflection.

The maze's outline contrasts with the lush lawn of Waterfront Park.

Visitors stop to observe the messages decorating the granite path.

Plan of the maze of Story Garden.

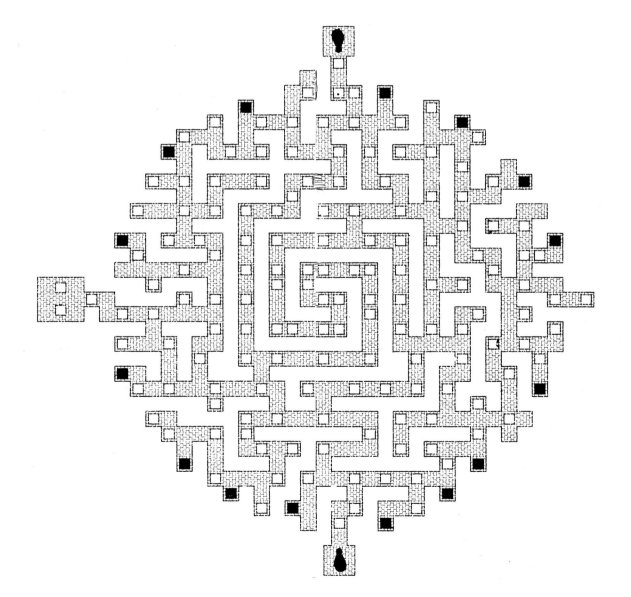

The monument is ringed with cubes.

The images on the path illustrate important moments in human life, relevant to everyone.

Detail showing two of the perimeter cubes.

Detail of one of the etched images.

BATTERY PARK CITY PAVILION

Demetri Porphyrios

Completion date: 1991

Location: Battery Park City, New York (USA)

Client/Promoter: Battery Park City Authority

Collaborators: Tor, Smolen, Callini and Anastos (structural engineers
and engineers of record)

The Battery Park City Pavilion is one of Demetri Porphyrios's most didactic projects. It shows a view of architecture that, contrary to the dominant tendencies of the last decades, puts forward the idea of classicism as an alternative contemporary architectural approach. The crisis that architecture is currently undergoing has highlighted, according to Porphyrios, the urgent need to re-examine the importance of tectonic representation as embodied in the principles of classicism.

Demetri Porphyrios, born in Athens in 1949, is internationally known for his academic and professional practice. He obtained his master's in Architecture and doctorate from the University of Princeton and has taught extensively in London and in the United States. For him, the architect's trade is inseparably linked to theoretical reflection. Porphyrios Associates, founded in London in 1981, have recently been involved in large projects like Belvedere Village (Ascot, UK), the Paternoster Offices (London), the new Quadrangle in Magdalen College, the Brindleyplace Offices (Bir-

Classical serenity contrast with Manhattan's abstraction.

mingham), and the extension of the city of Spetses (Greece). Porphyrios has also published many articles in international magazines, and his books include Sources of Modern Eclecticism, On the Methodology of Architectural History, Classicism is Not a Style, Classical Architecture, and D. Porphyrios: Buildings and Writings.

Battery Park City, situated against the high-tech background of the World Trade Center, draws immediate attention. Demetri Porphyrios clearly does not need this spectacular background to express his architectural views; however, the setting makes this small building seem even more daring and striking. To begin with there is an unexpected interaction of different scales. On the one hand, there is the overwhelmingly dominant scale of the towers; on the other hand, the intimate scale of what Porphyrios calls "a shelter", which in spite of its size acquires something of a monumental scale.

The pavilion is in fact both a shelter and a monument. Its floorplan consists of an atrium formed by four brick Doric columns and surrounded by a peristyle of 12 slender wooden columns. The rustic peristyle represents the idea of shelter, the "primitive hut", while the central patio affirms a more sophisticated architecture recalling classical antiquity.

The pavilion also functions as a belvedere. From the beginning, the site, situated at the cross-axis of two long vistas, suggested to the architect an airy, open structure. A stepped mound ensures there is a good view without obstructing city views for the passers-by. What has been created is a veritable "revealer of landscapes", encouraging reflection on the site's inherent visual relationships of which the architect was conscious

The pavilion has 12 slender wooden support posts with rustic proto-Ionic columns; they are supported on rough-cut stones and carry a perimeter timber architrave that in turn supports the roof's wooden rafters and boarding.

while formulating the initial design concept: that of civilization and nature (east-west axis, between the city and the countryside), and that of "commerce – industry and the inalienable human right of freedom" (the north-south axis, between the Empire State Building and the Statue of Liberty). Its visual transparency clearly exposes the building's constructional logic, in contrast with the elevational architecture of the World Trade Center.

Demetri Porphyrios is well versed in the art of construction, and here establishes a masterly balance between historical precedent and innovation. Flexibility in his use of language never results in trivial or gratuitous details (remaining faithful to his well-known dictum "classicism is not a style"). The a-canonical slender peristyle columns, for example, are an unusual but inventive extension of the traditional vocabulary.

In the "hyper-urban" cityscape that forms the pavilion's setting, the structure brings to life a whole range of opposing notions: craft and industrial standardisation, singularity and repetition, imitation and innovation, etc.. Whether by chance or by design, its plan, marked by the four solid central columns and delicate perystile, clearly recalls the organisational principle informing the plans of most skyscrapers, namely a stabilising central core and a thin external curtain-wall. Where the skyscraper concentrates its technological apparatus (lifts, ventilation, heating and air conditioning systems), the pavilion sites an open atrium, originally intended to contain a tree, and thereby defers to nature. The skyscraper embodies a universe of work conditioned by technological means, the physical translation of massive urbanisation generated by economic imperatives. In the pavilion, architecture objectifies its own origins in nature. In this res-

The stepped mound helps its role as a belvedere; it can also serve as a stage for public events such as open-air concerts.

Perspective view. In the background, on the right, the Empire State Building.

The four columns in the atrium are of brick with Doric stone capitals. It is not, however, a fully developed Doric order. The ungrooved column is of second-hand brick, and the Doric entablature is also missing.

Aerial view of south Manhattan. The pavilion (red dot) is in the North Park esplanade of New York's Battery Park City, between the River Hudson and the World Trade Center.

Sketch: a tree was originally planned for the centre of the pavilion to strengthen the evocation of the myth in which the original model for the Greek temple was the forest.

Elevation of pavilion.

View south-north.

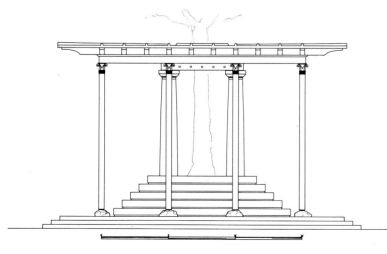

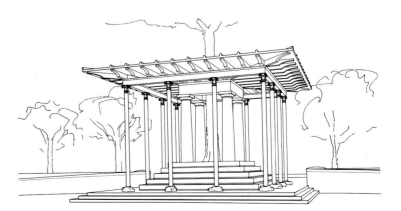

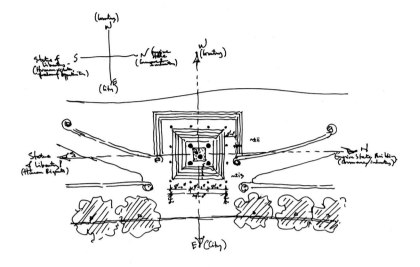

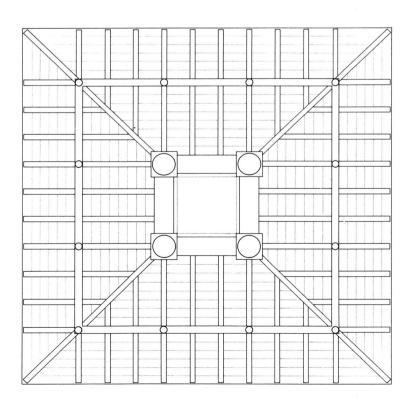

Preliminary sketch: the pavilion is at the crossing of two viewlines.

Plan of the roof: Porphyrios Associates's drawings are always distinguished by their high purity and precise draughtsmanship.

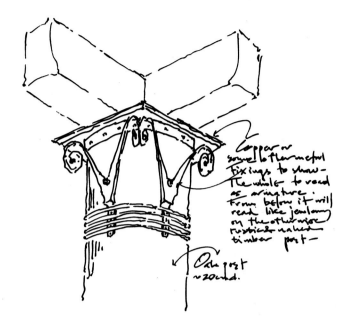 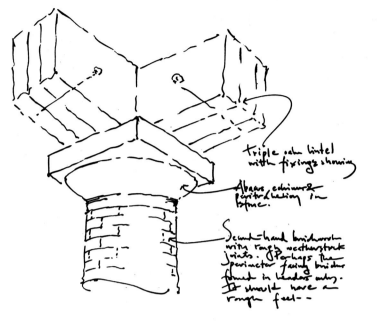

pect, architecture is here shown to be neither an arbitrary creation nor the inevitable outcome of straightforward building tech-
nique. Architecture, according to Porphyrios, is the mythical form
that man gives to his building craft through the principle of imitation of nature.

Through this and other works, Demetri Porphyrios seeks to
invoke not a nostalgia for the rusticity of pre-industrial cultures,
but to distance architectural discourse from certain prevalent
attitudes (like novelty for novelty's sake, temporality, and the
constant deferment to the high-tech technological icon), in
order to attain an "ontology of construction". Thoughts like these
may indeed provide genuine architectural alternatives for
modern society, especially in the context of growing global environmental problems.

Two details of the columns.

One of the sketches for the design that won the limited competition, in which Tod Williams Architects, USA, and Venturi Scott Brown and Associates, Inc., USA, also participated.

The contrast of scales; Porphyrios's pavilion's humility and the grandiloquence of the World Trade Center.

Battery Park City Pavilion, looking towards the city.

SCHIEDGRABEN UND HIRSCHGRABEN IN SCHWÄBISCH HALL

Wilfried Brückner

Completion date: 1990-1992

Location: Schwäbisch Hall, Baden-Württemberg (Germany)

Client/Promoter: Council of Schwäbisch Hall

Collaborators: Rolf Kronmüller (architect); Stiefel Engineering Office (planimetry); Volker Ellsäßer (landscape configuration); Edgar Gutbub and Michael Turzer (artistic collaboration)

The city of Schwäbisch Hall in south-west Germany, with more than 300,000 inhabitants, is thought to be the oldest industrial and manufacturing colony of Celtic origin. The city's architecture stands out for its historic city centre, with wooden-framed houses and a city wall with bridges and fortified towers. Since the city's founding, the cosmopolitan spirit of the well-off salt-traders and wine-merchants, together with the mint, created conditions that ensured the high quality of the city's architecture. Nowadays, the city continues to employ renowned architects and artists for its civic works, providing fresh input to the urban landscape.

The city's image has always been a mirror of the spiritual condition of its habitants. This forced the councillors to make an effort of imagination when planning the new layout of the Schiedgraben and Hirschgraben projects for parts of the fortress to the south and east of the city. The architect in charge of the

Schiedgraben: the steel bridge, with its delicate metal structure, and the city walls in the background.

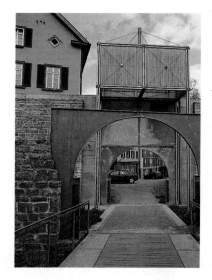

project was Wilfried Brückner, who was born in 1941 in Sternberg (in the former Czechoslovakia). He studied architecture between 1962 and 1968 at the Stuttgart Higher Technical School. From 1969 to 1975 he worked as an independent collaborator for the ROB design group in Stuttgart, and from 1975 to 1981 he practised as a town planner in Schwäbisch Hall. Since 1981 he has been the city's mayor, showing great enthusiasm in town planning and organisation.

His collaborators were the architects Rolf Kronmüller and Volker Ellsäßer from the Town-Planning Department, and Gerhard Regner and Helmut Harlaß, members of the Department of Civil Engineering. The other persons responsible for the Schiedgraben project were the metal constructions engineer Hugo Stiefel de Crailsheim and the sculptor Edgar Gutbub (Mannheim, 1940), a well-known local artist. The artistic contributions to the Hirschgraben project were by the sculptor Michael Turzer (Stuttgart, 1949).

Before the city's moat was uncovered, the area around the Schiedgraben drainage zone was landformed to create terraces, modified by the presence of a prison building and by a street crossing it. Major excavations were necessary to make the moat's course once more recognisable within the rolling fluvial landscape. There is now a modern steel bridge over the deep moat, sited on the remains of the pillars of a former stone bridge and forming a communication route between the mountains and the river valley. The ancient and modern construction materials create a balanced contrast. The impression of delicacy is mainly due to the bridge's steel grille covering, allowing observation of the excavations and also, if necessary, the passage of fire-fighting vehicles.

Schneewasserturm in Hirschgraben.

The native vegetation emerges between the ancient stones.

Stepped ramp between Lullenturm and Schneewasserturm.

The sculptures created by Gutbub for the top of the viaduct are allegories for the role of the bridge and the moat; the two constructions both separate and join, and this is represented by two pillars that confront each other, but which fit together and fuse perfectly. The sculptures' effect – separating or joining – depends on the position of the observer. The city's fort was thus not strictly speaking "rebuilt", but "built" as a functional architectural work by interpreting the pre-existing structures. The construction works were not limited to the bridge, but also included a complex of stairs on the ruined tower and a regular arrangement of the area around the walls surrounding the fortress. The materials and the construction type used establish a stimulating dialogue between the ancient and the modern. Traffic logistics required an underground garage for 224 vehicles under the hill; its cement roof was covered with soil and landscaped, so that the countryside could recover its original appearance.

For ecological reasons, a distinctly unconventional method of landforming and planting was chosen: rubble from the site and from other demolitions was collected and, after selection on the basis of ecological and shape factors, it was spread over the surface. This achieved reuse of the materials and will also support a diverse, dynamic and versatile flora.

Elsewhere on the river that crosses Schwäbisch Hall the challenge was different: completing the outermost of the city's inner ringroads required the design and construction of a new bypass, but one that did not clash with or isolate the residential area next to the Baindtgasse. The requirement for it to be sunken below ground level suggested making a virtue of necessity, i.e., using the excavations to recover the historic towers, city walls and the

Steel constructions on the city wall: a reminder of the former towers.

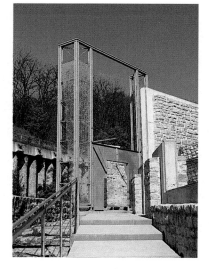

walls of the moats. The intrinsically fascinating remains of the ancient fortifications form a wonderful backdrop for future artistic events. Two former defensive constructions are joined together by a ramp starting inside the city wall, while the works in steel designed by the sculptor Turzer and the architect rise above the ruins. The heavy natural feeling of the stone is attenuated by the transparency and the technical perfection of the steel, so the observer feels both the horizontal tranquillity and the vertical growth. The continuity of the moat and the high walls of uncut stone is broken by the modern construction elements, with steel stairs, gates and sheds crossing through the setting framed by the ruined towers. The towers' bases consist of the ashlars of the original walls, while the transition to the base of the steel construction consists of layers of treated stone. A tall work in steel bars forms a figure with aeronautical overtones, partially covered in perforated sheet metal and planking in different coloured varnishes. The structures form rhythmic points along the overall setting of the city walls. The aesthetic effect complements the functionality of this architectural work, which uses its valuable historical heritage and develops it in accordance with the original intentions.

The metal structures remind us of the location of the former city walls.

Detail of the ramp of stairs in Hirschgraben.

Wall of the Hirschgraben moat: inner wall, outer wall and the city wall.

Transition from the old city wall to the new one.

Schiedgraben Bridge; the metal structure rests on the old pillars.

Location of Schiedgraben and Hirschgraben in Schwäbisch Hall; aerial photo.

Central perspective from the west.

General plan of the city wall in Schiedgraben.

Schiedgraben; ground plan of the bridge.

Lullentor in Hirschgraben; front view.

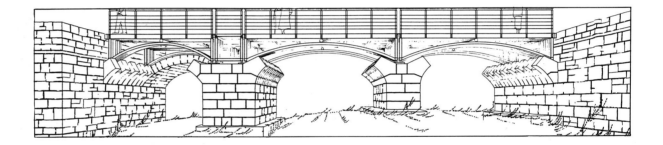

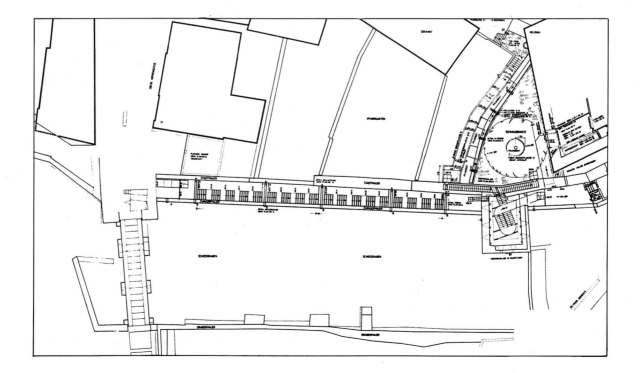

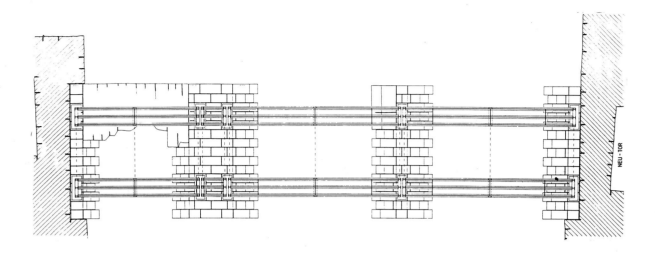

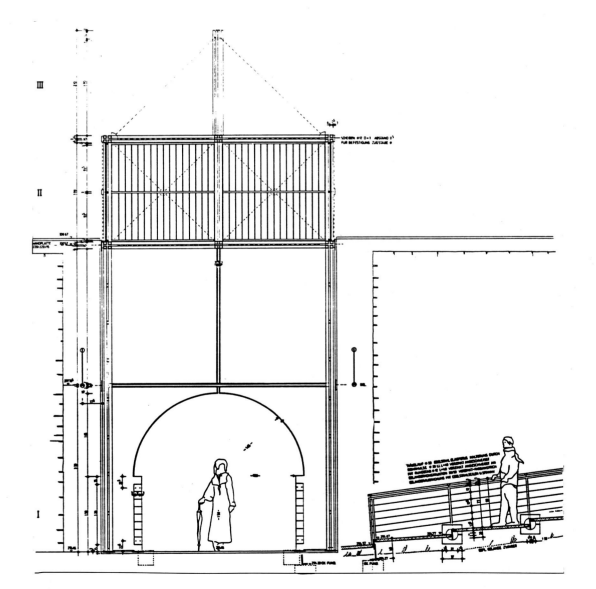

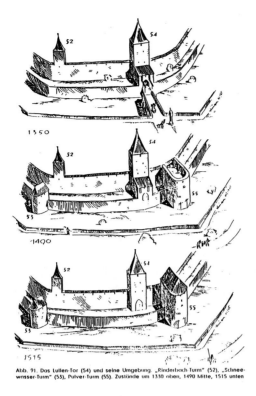

Abb. 91. Das Lullen-Tor (54) und seine Umgebung. „Rinderbach-Turm" (52), „Schnee-wasser-Turm" (53), Pulver-Turm (55). Zustände um 1350 oben, 1490 Mitte, 1515 unten

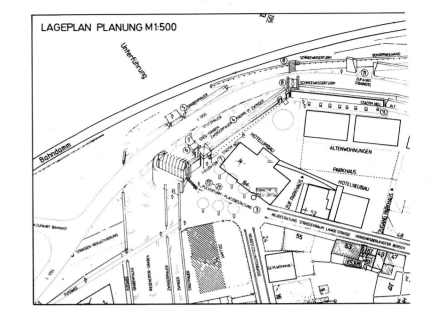

Pulver-Turm (55) und Lullen-Tor (54) von Südost nach Zeichnung von Louis Braun 1847.

Lullentor (54) and its surroundings, Rinderbachturm (52), Schneewasser-turm (53), Pulwerturm (55); as in 1515.

In the foreground, the steel construction showing the site of the former defence tower.

Axonometric projection of Hirschgraben and general layout (1992).

Schiedgraben; ground plan of the bridge.

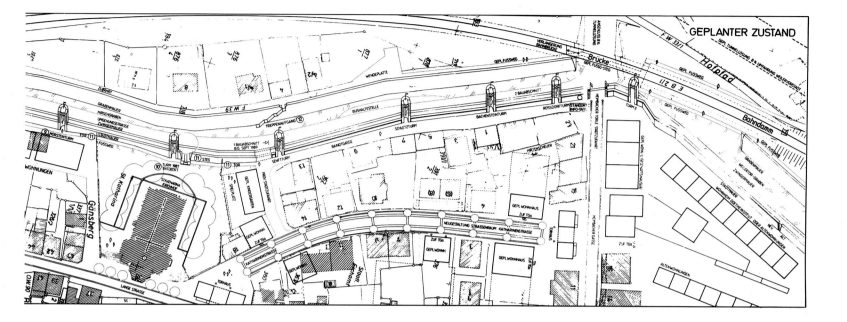

VOIE SUISSE.
L'ITINÉRAIRE GENEVOIS

Georges Descombes

On the shores of Lake Uri, the XIX-century Axenstrasse promoted the transformation of the region by developing the villages between Brunnen and Flüelen.

Completion date: May, 1991

Location: Lake Uri (Switzerland)

Client/Promoter: État de Genève

Collaborators: Cyrille Chatelain and Bernard Spichiger (botanists); André Coboz (historian of urban development); Hervé Cauville (writer and art critic); Alain Léveillé (architect and urban designer); François-Yves Morin (art critic); Maurice Pianzola (art historian); Bernard Tottet (geographer); Raymond Schaffert (architect and urban designer); Jean-Pierre Cêtre (civil engineer)

La Voie Suisse is a 35-km-long pedestrian path around Lake Uri whose conditioning and layout was the result of collaboration between all 26 cantons of the Swiss Confederation. Each of the cantons took responsibility for one part of the route, but without losing sight of the overall plan as a whole. The length of the stretch assigned to each canton was proportional to its number of inhabitants, in this case corresponding to the two kilometres that separate Morschach from Brunnen. The Swiss architect Georges Descombes was commissioned to perform the studies and design the scheme, which was planned between 1987 and 1990 and performed in 1990 and 1991.

Georges Descombes (Geneva, 1939) graduated as an archi-

tect from the École d'Architecture et Urbanisme de Genève in 1969, and he then worked for people such as Nervi, Beaudouin and Saugey. Afterwards he also graduated from the Architectural Association Graduate School (1973). Two years later he returned to his home town, where he now combines his work as an architect with teaching. His two best-known projects, the park in Lancy and his design for the Geneva section of the Voie Suisse, have been published in prestigious international publications and have received widespread critical and public approval.

The long list of specialists who took part in Geneva's design meant that a thorough analysis of the site was possible, and so the design could really respond to the site's distinctive features. The result of all this work was also published in a book, Voie Suisse. L'itinéraire genevois. De Morschach à Brunnen, in 1991, which in Descombes' opinion is closely related to the project as a whole.

The contribution by Carmen Perrin to the Voie Suisse. Erratic boulder.

The small works along the route of the forest paths raise questions about blandness, questions about the surroundings.

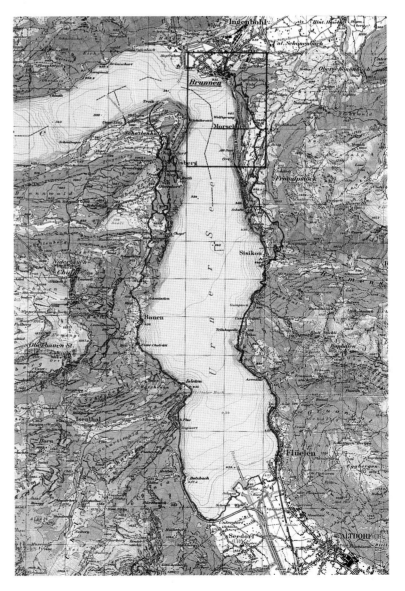

Plan of Lake Uri, with the route of the Voie Suisse, and the Geneva route.

Erratic boulders.

The Chänzeli Belvedere: detail.

View of the surroundings.

The design had to fulfil its purpose, which was to follow a safe route with a good view, but it was also based on a central idea: to encourage people to understand more clearly what the site used to be and now is, and to show it by means of carefully planned designs. The idea was thus to awaken the landscape, heal it and offer it to the public. The scheme included a wide range of different types of features. Sometimes the aim was to preserve the landscape but care was taken not to reduce access for walkers; steep slopes were negotiated by installing with gradins of wood and grass where people can sit and look at the countryside or continue up to the higher areas. On other occasions the desire was to make the site more interesting: this is the context in which to understand the musician Max Neuhaus' creation of a sound installation, using loudspeakers in a clearing in the wood to reproduce the forest's hidden life, thus changing our perception of the site and our behaviour within it. The long-term aim was to recover the site's history, for example by restoring a crumbling xix-century wall, a belvedere and some rainfall runoff drainage channels.

The Chänzeli Belvedere has a more "artificial" and radical design, with a circular metal structure around a lime tree, a railing and two benches. The two concentric circles of the metal

framework break up the view of the surrounding landscape while the opening overlooking the lake draws the visitor's gaze towards the desired point: the belvedere's purpose is thus reinforced.

There were also other original collaborations such as the one by Carmen Perrin, who took an interest in the erratic stones (till) left behind by the movement of glaciers. She performed an "archaeological" study and cleaned them of vegetation; by doing this she assigned them the status of historic monuments. Richard Long built seven tumuli of 100 stones each, which he later spread along the lake's shoreline. Some of his thoughts from 1982 are especially applicable to the works on the shores of Lake Uri: "These works are an emanation of the site itself, they are its recomposition and, with time, the site will once again absorb them; my urge is to work for the site, not against it."

In 1991, after the conclusion of the celebrations of the seventh centenary of the Swiss Confederation, many of the ephemeral features of this and the other canton's projects' disappeared; the vegetation once more took possession of the site, but a definite trace was left, waiting to be rediscovered on a future occasion.

Different views of the small interventions along the Voie Suisse´route.
Also, two views of the past.

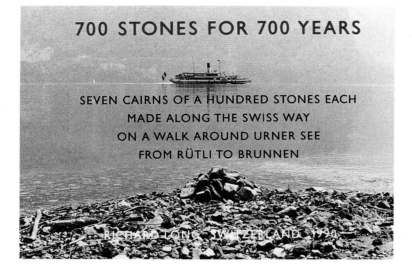

700 STONES FOR 700 YEARS

SEVEN CAIRNS OF A HUNDRED STONES EACH
MADE ALONG THE SWISS WAY
ON A WALK AROUND URNER SEE
FROM RÜTLI TO BRUNNEN

RICHARD LONG SWITZERLAND 1990

Richard Long built seven tumuli, each with a 100 stones, along the route.

Sketch of the Chänzeli Belvedere.

As one enters the wood's wooded grove, one encounters a high bright sound — like a fine aural mist. It permeates the grove, seeming to come from nowhere.

At first the sound seems constant, but if one listens for a few minutes an inner detail and motion begin to appear. After a while the sound sometimes seems to disappear, becoming imbedded in the sound of the woods. It is an intense but not unpleasant place to be.

Upon leaving the wood the sound becomes distant and things slip back to normal.

MAX NEUHAUS

BRUNNEN WOODSMOKE
MOSS
STUMP
ERRATIC
A HUNDRED STONES
SHRINE

PUDDLE

WEDDING

RÜTLI
SQUIRREL
WORKBENCH
ANTS
FORK AND RAKE

SHADY

POPPIES

PINE BARK
HAWK
LILAC
CAT CREAK
WOODPECKERS

RUSHING WATER
DUSTY HAT
WARM ROCK
ZIG-ZAG
A HUNDRED STONES
BEETLE
LIZARD
POPPING EARS
LAPPING WATER
ASHES
CHIMES
DUCKLING

A HUNDRED STONES
ECHO
A HUNDRED STONES
SWIFTS
DRIPPING WATER
PINES
COOL
ROAR
MIDDAY

BUTTERFLY
A HUNDRED STONES

WINDY

STRATA

WHITE HORSES

BEACH FIRES

MOWN GRASS
A HUNDRED STONES
A HUNDRED STONES
DRIFTWOOD
STRAIGHT FLOW
HAY RICK

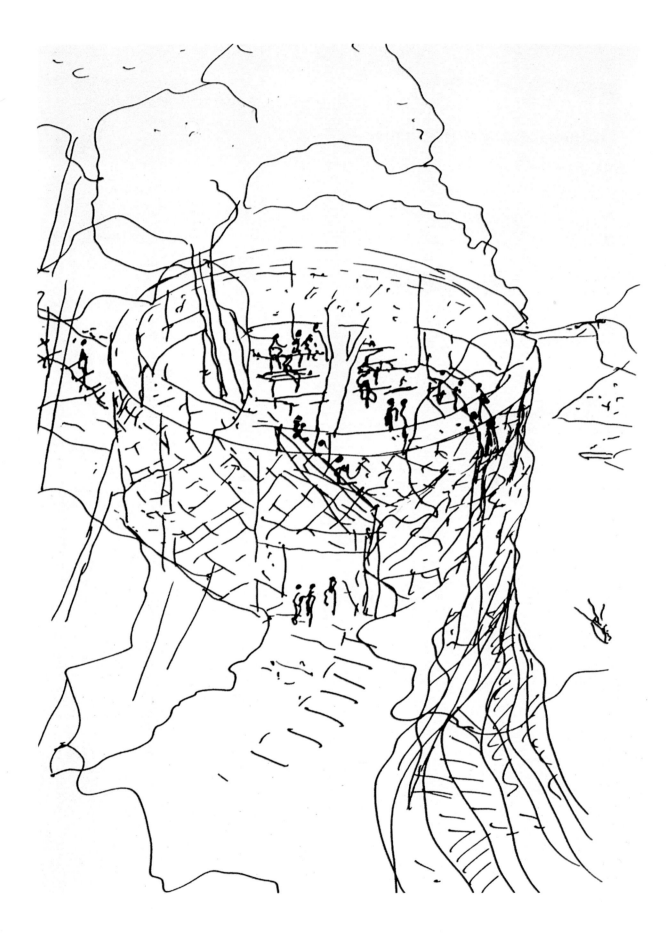

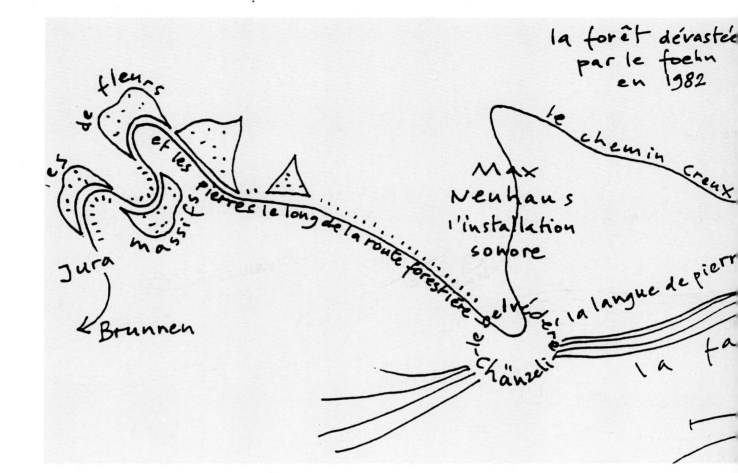

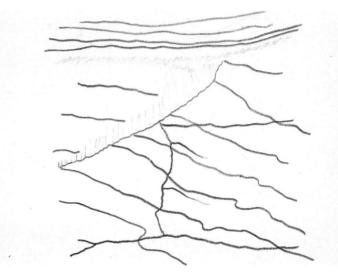

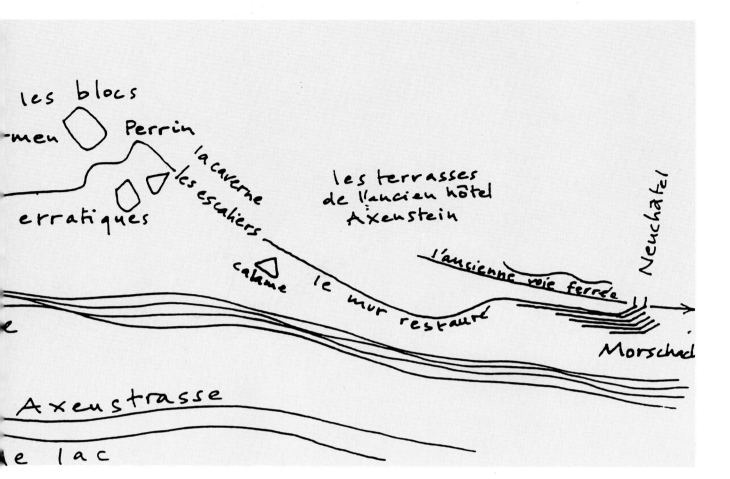

les blocs

men   Perrin

erratiques   la caverne   les escaliers   les terrasses de l'ancien hôtel Axenstein

calame   le mur restauré   l'ancienne voie ferrée   Neuchâtel

Morschad

Axenstrasse

e lac

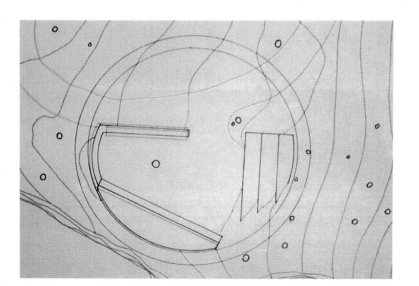

Plans of the route.

Plan of the Belvedere.